The Endpoint Security Paradox

Realising implementation success

Andrew Avanessian

The Endpoint Security Paradox
Realising implementation success

Credits

Author: Andrew Avanessian

Reviewers: James Maude, Senior Security Engineer & Laura Butler, Head of Content

Dedicated to Simon Avanessian

About the Author

Andrew established the consultancy and technology services at a global endpoint security company Avecto. He regularly provides security and technology advice to large enterprises, overseeing software deployments across millions of endpoints. His background in IT infrastructure ensures he can clearly translate complex requirements, finding technical solutions to commercial challenges. With a keen interest in cyber security and the end user experience, Andrew is a regular contributor to press articles and has spoken at numerous security and technology events. He has also appeared on the BBC and CNBC News channels.

Andrew holds an Honors degree in Computer Science, together with a number of industry recognized qualifications from Microsoft, Apple and CompTIA. These include Microsoft MCP, MCSA, MCSE, ITIL.

Preface

Having worked with thousands of clients, from SMBs to truly global enterprises, the one thing that constantly troubles me is that companies (large or small), never seem to truly understand WHY they are embarking on their latest security project.

I am not saying the IT teams involved do not have any goals; of course they do. However, it is often the case that they do not take a holistic view of their IT environment or projects, letting technology drive the objectives, and not the business need. Businesses need to start with the end in mind, or in other words, the "why?" So before you start, ask yourself these questions:

1. Why are we running this project?
2. Do we really understand the requirements?
3. Have we asked the business owners what they need?
4. What benefit will we gain by doing this?

If you cannot truly answer these questions then you should go back to the drawing board, as ploughing ahead can result in poorly designed and implemented solutions. Putting this in to context with my experiences in the IT security field, lack of answers has led to the "Swiss Cheese" effect – essentially IT security systems full of holes! There are literally thousands of large enterprises that spend millions of dollars on IT security, and yet they are still breached.

IT security is not a dark art! You do not need the latest and greatest analysis tools or frameworks, and you do not even have to have a deep understanding of all the attack vectors that exist. You simply need to get the foundations right. Would you go out and leave your front door wide open or give your online banking details to all your acquaintances? No, you wouldn't… but yet I am often astounded at how many organisations do exactly this when it comes to IT security. They get the basics wrong and they are breached, they throw money at the problem (not fully understanding it) and poorly implement the latest widget or appliance to hopefully "detect" the cyber-criminals. At the time of writing a famous movie production company has just suffered a major breach, which could have been easily prevented by getting the security foundations right. **Detection does not work and yes, prevention is possible!**

You will always, always, (yes always) be two or more steps behind the cyber criminals. They do not have funding cycles; they do not operate change management windows. They simply spend all their time adapting the malware payloads. Detecting these threats is impossible! If you analyse the big headline breaches in the press today, I guarantee over 95% could be prevented by getting the basics rights.

So why am I writing this book?

After years of seeing IT projects fail and disaster after disaster play out in the media, I'm writing this book to share my experiences in the IT security field, specifically focusing on implementation success and best practices, to help improve organisational protection. I want to overcome some of the myths and cut through the noise to ensure businesses don't needlessly fall prey to attack.

 A best practice is a process or methodology learned through experience that can provide predictable, desired results.

This book brings together my knowledge of deploying endpoint security (on both desktops and servers) to millions of endpoints across thousands of companies, including some of the largest on the planet.

For me, the biggest issue facing endpoint security projects is the tradeoff between security and usability. Both ends of the spectrum are easy to achieve. However, the balance between those seemingly polarized opposites is not!

The book is split into two distinct halves. Firstly, we will look at security principles and pitfalls. I am not going to detail threat vectors and techniques for analysing the attack chain, because there are hundreds of books out there doing that. However, I will provide a high-level overview of common attack vectors for completeness and setting the context. The topics covered in this book will help to ensure the security foundations are laid correctly, in the context of a defence in depth strategy, whilst still enabling user freedom.

In the second half, we will cover best practices for design, planning and implementation success. The implementation methodology used here has been tried and tested across hundreds of diverse organisations. I will look at the challenges and considerations, and help you build a plan for success.

The principles discussed here apply generically to successful projects, not just security. Obviously, every organisation has a unique set of challenges but the desired result is common to all. Success! There are many ways to achieve this and this book will provide an implementation methodology, which is proven to be robust and secure in the most demanding of environments.

Contents

Preface v

PART ONE
SECURITY PRINCIPLES AND PITFALLS 2

1 The ever-changing threat landscape 4
    1.1. Summary: Let's get proactive 14

2 Security foundations 16
    2.1. Least privilege security – the best place to start 16
    2.2. Application control (AKA whitelisting) 19
    2.3. Use of standard, secure system configurations 19
    2.4. Patch application and system software 20
    2.5. Defence in depth still works – don't just take my word for it 20
    2.6. Summary: A word of caution – there is no silver bullet! 23

3 Good advice is hard to follow 24
    3.1. 100% security or 100% freedom? That is the question 25
    3.2. Why is 100% freedom a challenge? 27
    3.3. Why is 100% security a challenge? 29
    3.4. Operating costs – you cannot win! 33
    3.5. Perception becomes reality 35
    3.6. Summary: User experience is king 37

4 Why typical tools fall short 40
    4.1. Least privilege – typical tools and tech 41
    4.2. Application whitelisting – typical tools and tech 78
    4.3. Standard Secure Configurations – typical tools and tech 90
    4.4. Patching – typical tools and tech 93

PART TWO
TECHNOLOGY TO ACHIEVE DEFENCE IN DEPTH 97

5 Protection that works 98
  5.1. Setting foundations with privilege management.................. 101
  5.2. Focus on secure, standard configuration 104
  5.3. Application control is easy (trust me!) 105
  5.4. Detection is dead – sort of 108
  5.5. Patch, patch! Oh - and patch!... 112
  5.6. Sandboxing - let's not forget about zero day exploits 113
  5.7. Endpoint behavioural analysis 117
  5.8. Summary - perceptions of defence in depth...................... 119

6 Defence in Depth and your bottom line 123
  6.1. Security recommendations from external experts.............. 124
  6.2. Don't believe me? Try it for yourself! 127

PART THREE
IMPLEMENTATION SUCCESS 131

**7 Defence in Depth is great in theory –
  but how do I implement it?....................................... 132**
  7.1. The implementation methodology 133
  7.2. Stage 1 – Design workshop (start with the end in mind) 135
  7.3. Stage 2 – Technology deployment 148
  7.4. Stage 3 – Requirements discovery
       (understanding your use case)....................................... 151
  7.5. Stage 4 – Data analysis & use case definition.................... 157
  7.6. Stage 5 – Layering policies 165
  7.7. Stage 6 – Policy testing 172
  7.8. Stage 7 – Internal communication.....................................176
  7.9. Stage 8 – Production deployment 180

8	Building group consensus	188
9	Tools and vendor selection	193
	9.1. Security	194
	9.2. Features	195
	9.3. Ease of use	196
	9.4. Architecture	197
	9.5. Support	198
	9.6. Innovation	198
	9.7. Vendor selection questions	199
10	Final thoughts	210

1

PART ONE

Security Principles and Pitfalls

1	The ever-changing threat landscape	4
2	Security foundations	16
3	Good advice is hard to follow	24
4	Why typical tools fall short	40

CHAPTER 1
The ever-changing threat landscape

1.1. Summary: Let's get proactive   14

Over recent years, the news has often been dominated by headlines detailing the irrevocable damage caused by cybercrime and insider attacks. Cybercrime is now a trillion dollar industry and has an increasingly low barrier to entry. The amount of valuable data stored digitally has also skyrocketed, making the rewards on offer for cyber criminals huge. Unsurprisingly, it has attracted the attention of everyone from organised crime units to nation states looking to conduct cyber-espionage.

Every day we create 2.5 quintillion bytes of data and by 2020, the amount of data stored will be 50x larger than today.[1] Yet in Q4 2015, McAfee recorded 327 new threats per minute or more than five every second,[2] meaning the threat level and potential for damage to an organisation is astronomical.

---

1   http://www.testpoint.com.au/blog/by-2020-the-total-amount-of-data-stored-is-expected-to-be-50x-larger-than-today/)
2   http://www.mcafee.com/uk/resources/reports/rp-quarterly-threats-nov-2015.pdf

THE EVER-CHANGING THREAT LANDSCAPE

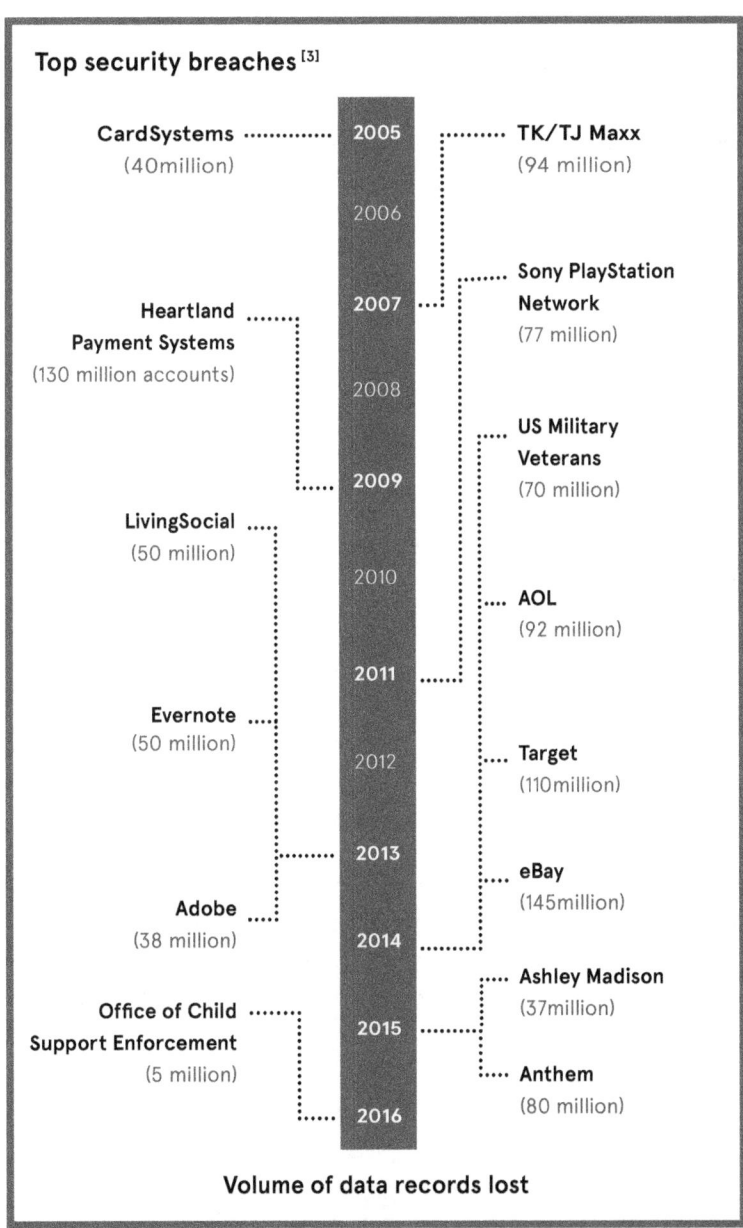

Top security breaches [3]

CardSystems (40million)	2005 · TK/TJ Maxx (94 million)
	2006
Heartland Payment Systems (130 million accounts)	2007 · Sony PlayStation Network (77 million)
	2008
	2009 · US Military Veterans (70 million)
LivingSocial (50 million)	2010
	2011 · AOL (92 million)
Evernote (50 million)	2012 · Target (110million)
	2013
Adobe (38 million)	2014 · eBay (145million)
Office of Child Support Enforcement (5 million)	2015 · Ashley Madison (37million) · Anthem (80 million)
	2016

Volume of data records lost

---

3   http://www.informationisbeautiful.net/visualizations/worlds-biggest-data-breaches-hacks/
    http://247wallst.com/technology-3/2016/04/15/2016-data-breaches-added-5-million-exposed-records-last-week/

The Target breach is a prime example of this. According to its earnings report, in just eight months the retail chain's profits fell 62% following attack, shareholders lost $148 million,[4] and in a significant effort to reverse the destruction, $150 million was spent. Yet the breach could have been avoid by getting the basics right!

Threats are not just coming from outside sources either. The scandal involving Edward Snowden - in which the computer expert and former CIA employee disclosed thousands of classified documents belonging to the NSA as a contractor for consulting firm Booz Allen Hamilton – highlights the need for internal security as well as external. Again, these breaches could have been avoided with simple security principles.

But what does this all mean? There is so much hype in the cyber security space, with attack vector acronyms being discussed on a daily basis. More often than not, this serves to strike fear into the hearts of the average IT professional. We know that cybercrime inflicts pain on organisations and that as hacking methods become more sophisticated, the cybercrime economy is booming. But beyond these certainties, there's significant confusion around what types of cybercrime exist and how to identify them.

There is no doubt that breaches exact a costly toll on victims, in terms of both time and money. These hidden costs often do not appear as line items on financial statements for a number of reasons. First, the costs are often indirect, resulting in wasted resources and missed opportunities. Second, organisations are incentivised to downplay the effects of cybercrime to avoid unwanted attention from the public and media.

---

4   http://qz.com/252466/target-customers-havent-forgiven-it-for-that-data-breach/

The cost of data breaches due to malicious or criminal attacks increased from an average of $159 in 2014 to $170 per record in 2015. Last year, these attacks represented 42% of root causes of a data breach, and this increased to 47% of root causes in 2015[5]

This price tag includes the costs incurred in detecting and responding to a breach, notifying victims, conducting post-response support, and lost business. Clearly, data breaches are financially burdensome on the organisations experiencing them.

In addition to these financial losses, organisations also suffer from lost time. Depending on the type of incident they experience, businesses may lose days, weeks, or even months of time to incident-response activities.

According to the 2015 Ponemon Cost of Cyber Crime report, the average cost to organisations is $15m – up from $3.8m in 2010.

In the following sections I'll take a look at some of the attack vectors to help put into context what we need to protect against.

---

5   2015 Cost of a Data Breach Study, IBM/The Ponemon Institute, May 2015

THE ENDPOINT SECURITY PARADOX

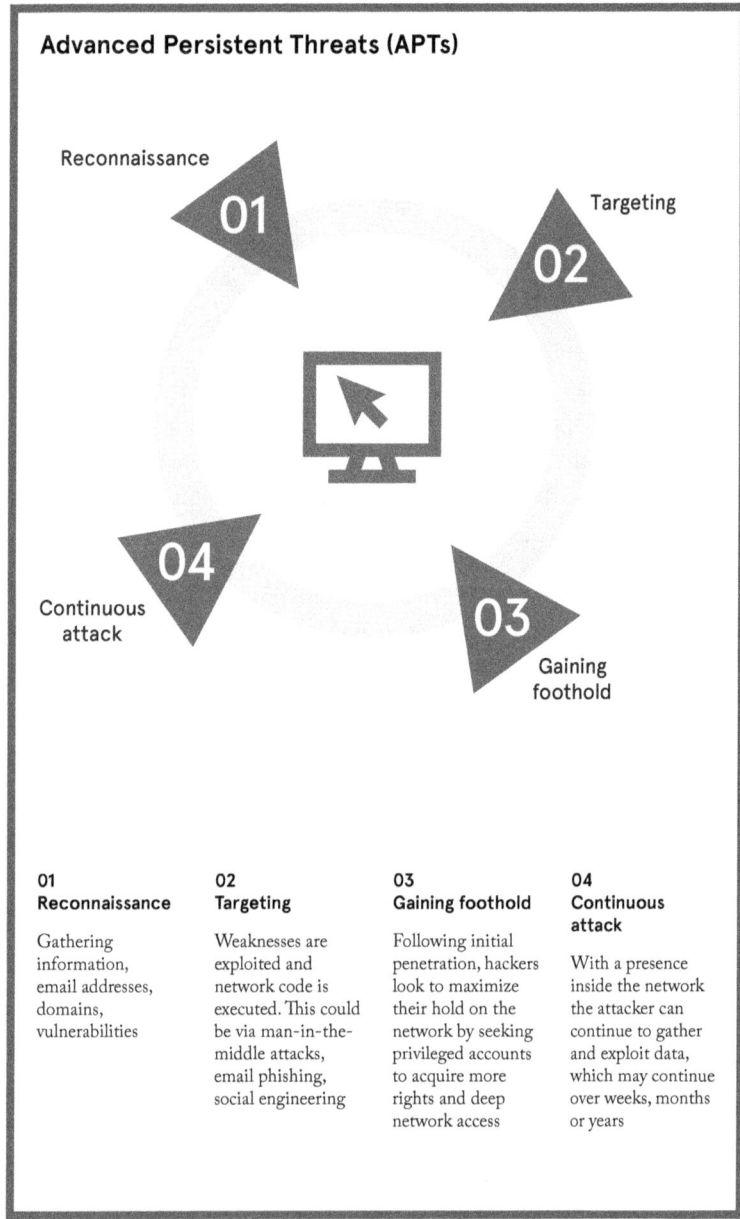

Advanced Persistent Threats (APTs)

01 Reconnaissance

Gathering information, email addresses, domains, vulnerabilities

02 Targeting

Weaknesses are exploited and network code is executed. This could be via man-in-the-middle attacks, email phishing, social engineering

03 Gaining foothold

Following initial penetration, hackers look to maximize their hold on the network by seeking privileged accounts to acquire more rights and deep network access

04 Continuous attack

With a presence inside the network the attacker can continue to gather and exploit data, which may continue over weeks, months or years

An APT is a long-term sophisticated threat launched against a specific target, with considerable technical capabilities and resources. Traditional security strategies are unable to fight against ATPs, which can run over years and use multiple vectors. Crucially, attackers are organised and motivated.

In Ponemon's 2015 State of the Endpoint report, 65% of respondents stated that APTs are frequently seen in their organisation's network – one of the biggest increases in noted threats.[6]

Targeted malware

Targeted malware is a type of malware destined for one specific organisation or industry. These are of particular concern because they are designed to capture sensitive information and are unique to the organisation. They utilise vectors such as spear phishing emails, vulnerable unpatched services or zero day exploits—to name but a few—against line of business applications, such as Office.

Phishing

Phishing is the process of sending malicious emails that appear to be legitimate, often spoofing email addresses from reputable organisations. Commonly they are trying to trick users into running malware, leaking sensitive information or performing financial transactions. According to McAfee, 80% of users are unable to spot phishing emails.[7]

Zero days

Zero day attacks mean that a previously unknown vulnerability is exploited before the vendor has released a patch. This is dangerous when research shows that 99.9% of the exploited vulnerabilities in 2015 had been compromised more than a year after the associated CVE was published.[8]

---

6 http://www.ponemon.org/blog/2015-state-of-the-endpoint-report-user-centric-risk
7 http://www.mcafee.com/uk/about/news/2014/q3/20140904-01.aspx
8 http://www.verizonenterprise.com/uk/DBIR/2015/

Hackers are getting more sophisticated too. In 2015 there were seven noted zero day attacks, including an exploit in Hancom's Hangul Word Processor by North Korean threat actors and the Microsoft Office Zero-Day CVE-2015-2424 leveraged by Tsar Team.

Unpatched software

Unpatched software is classed as that which has vulnerabilities that have yet to be fixed by automatic updates. This can turn a zero day threat into a forever day exploit if the relevant patch isn't added.

In 2015, F-Secure found that 70% of businesses are leaving themselves vulnerable to attacks by failing to patch their software.

This is further compounded by End of Life (EOL) software such as Windows XP or older versions of Internet Explorer, which will no longer be patched by Microsoft. EOL software is often found running in corporate environments long after the vendor has stopped supporting it. This is mainly due to compatibility issues with Line of Business (LOB) applications, that were never designed to run with the latest versions and are too expensive to redevelop. These applications and their associated browser plugins pose a serious security concern.

Insider threats

In addition to external cyber threats, organisations need to be aware of threats from the inside, which can be even harder to protect against, as highlighted by the case of Edward Snowden in 2013. Vormetric's 2015 Insider Threat Report found that 59% of companies in the US consider privileged users to be the greatest threat to their organisation, with 93% claiming they are somewhat or more vulnerable to insider threats.[9]

---

9   http://www.vormetric.com/campaigns/insiderthreat/2015/pdf/2015-vormetric-insider-threat-pr-v2.pdf

When insider attacks are malicious, the individual is likely to be one step ahead of external threat actors because they already know what the company's assets are and how to gain access to them for the purpose of theft, disclosure or destruction.

Meanwhile, according to Ponemon's 2015 Cost of Data Breach study, 25% of data breaches are caused by human error, taking an average of 158 days to identify.[10]

Social engineering

Malware and social engineering are the same; exploit someone/something, remain undetected and gain access. In 1995 Kevin Mitnik was arrested for penetrating some of the most well-guarded systems in the world, including the likes of Sun Microsystems, Digital Equipment Corporation, Motorola, Netcom, and Nokia. So what was the weapon of choice for the FBI's most wanted hacker? Social engineering. Kevin had learned at an early age that people were a great resource and could be manipulated for information and access.

Fast forward 20 years and what have we learnt? Surprisingly little. The Aircraft part manufacturer FACC was recently tricked into transferring over $50m to a Chinese Agricultural Bank; Amazon has been socially engineered into giving away customers' personal details. Belgian Bank Crelan lost $75.8m to a fake CEO. Overall, the FBI attributed $1.2bn of losses globally to social engineering fraud in the past two years.[11]

Ultimately, the best security in the world can be bypassed with social engineering, because the user is the weakest link in the chain. In IT we often create heroes, all powerful beings, omnipresent on the network with power over the life and death of data and running processes.

---

10 http://www-03.ibm.com/security/data-breach/
11 http://www.ft.com/cms/s/0/83b4e9be-db16-11e5-a72f-1e7744c66818.html#axzz46NaYmanF

In reality they are human, they are fallible and therefore they can still fall into the same social engineering traps as anyone else. There's just something about the digital world that renders many blind. For instance, in a bank we don't give the branch manager keys to the building, the code for the vault and leave him to it. There is audit, time released locks and clearly defined access procedures. This prevents attackers from easily engineering their way in. Maybe they can dress as an "IT guy" and get behind the counter, but the multiple layers of defence should stop them getting to the vault. However, when it comes to our digital wealth of data and IP we often have people at junior levels holding the key to the vault with varying degrees of accountability.

Organisations are not always switched on to this when it comes to their digital wealth of data and IP. Physical and digital defences need to work together. A denial-of-service (DoS) attack is often used to distract from financial fraud or data breaches. Ransomware and malware can trick or pressure users into revealing passwords or financial information. Often employees assume that social engineering is limited to emails asking for monetary donations, such as those from Nigerian royalty, and can easily be avoided. But even Nigerian phishing emails are more sophisticated than they appear, serving as an efficient way to target "Mugu" (fools).

Digital access

In digital we talk about defence in depth (DiD) but rarely do we implement this for people. To break into an organisation from a computer we might need to bypass firewalls, avoid IDS, find a vulnerable machine, create an exploit, avoid detections, pivot and move laterally to reach the target endpoint. Far from a trivial task. To socially engineer our way in we might simply have to ask the target user to "have a look at this invoice", "click this link" or simply call them up and say "Mark from accounts needs to know X".

Physical access

When we think of digital attacks, we often think of a hacker in a remote location. However, physical intrusions also happen, whether they originate from inside or outside an organisation.

Take a second to think about how often we open doors to strangers in our respective work spaces. We have no way of knowing their intent but we would consider it rude to ask them. Yet there's nothing to say they're not carrying a USB stick containing malware that will bypass all network defences and be plugged directly into an endpoint.

It's a similar situation when dealing with employees. Organisations need to give staff enough access to documents to allow them to remain productive and prevent situations where they're constantly having to ask for permissions. However, in doing so, they leave themselves vulnerable.

Exploit kits

An interesting development in recent years is the introduction of exploit kits. These are toolkits that cybercriminals use to build malware attacks on the fly. Several kits have since been developed then sold or rented out like commercial products in underground markets.

A typical exploit kit usually provides a management console and preloaded vulnerabilities that make it easier for a cybercriminal to launch an attack. Exploit kits also provide a user interface for the person who controls them, which typically includes information on success rates and other types of statistics. Malware creation is now an industry in itself, with supportable software tools to help create new attacks and, worst of all, it will only get easier.

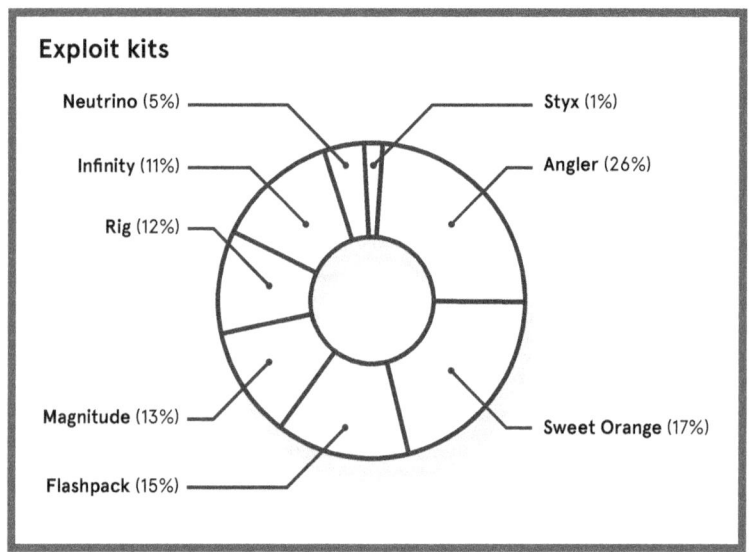

1.1. Summary: Let's get proactive

Reactive security strategies alone are no longer enough to overcome today's next generation threats. Cyber criminals are constantly evolving threats and approaches, making it impossible to detect a threat – even those that have only slightly been modified. When decoded, we can clearly see that today's cyber criminals are actually using old techniques and approaches, which are modified and sewed together with new attacks.

With more and more attacks taking place, traditional security measures, such as antivirus, monitoring/session recording and passwords are not enough when used in isolation. Detection approaches simply do not work! You will always be two to three steps behind the cyber criminals. However, by layering multiple strategies it is possible to create a balanced security architecture.

Attitudes towards security also need to be changed. Fundamentally, security is a culture that everyone has to buy into and we should not differentiate between the endpoint and the employee. Good security principles still apply. Without these in place, we leave gaps that can be socially engineered and exploited.

Time and time again I see security vendors offering the latest widget or system that is going to "save the world". However, there is no silver bullet when it comes to overcoming cyber challenges. Securing your systems against the latest cyber attacks is not rocket science. Likewise, when people talk about stopping the cyber criminals getting inside, it is simply not enough. Ensuring you have perimeter defences is important, but the traditional eggshell approach to security (where the outsides are hard but the insides are soft) is not enough and also a bit 90s – more on this later.

Yes, there are always new zero day exploits uncovered, but I will be explaining how the right security foundations can thwart these attacks. I will also be sharing industry expert advice, which backs up these techniques.

Remember where your data is stored! Your organisation's IP is on the endpoint, whether that be a desktop or server. The weakest link is your end users and these will be targeted.

CHAPTER 2
Security foundations

2.1.	Least privilege security – the best place to start!	16
2.2.	Application control (AKA whitelisting)	19
2.3.	Use of standard, secure system configurations	19
2.4.	Patch application and system software	20
2.5.	Don't take my word for it!	20
2.6.	Summary—A word of caution—there is no silver bullet!	23

In this chapter, we'll take a look at some key security principles that form the foundations of any successfully security model. I will also cross-reference advice provided by organisations such as SANS, GCHQ and many more.

2.1. Least privilege security – the best place to start

Least privilege security is the practice of assigning users and programs the least permissions required to complete a given task.

The Department of Defense Trusted Computer System Evaluation Criteria, (DOD-5200.28-STD), also known as the Orange Book, defines least privilege as a principle that "requires that each subject in a system be granted the most restrictive set of privileges (or lowest clearance) needed for the performance of authorised tasks. The application of this principle limits the damage that can result from accident, error, or unauthorised use." [11]

Least privilege was first put forward as a design principle by Jerry Saltzer and Mike Schroeder over 30 years ago. According to Saltzer and Schroeder:

"Every program and every user of the system should operate using the least set of privileges necessary to complete the job. Primarily, this principle limits the damage that can result from an accident or error. It also reduces the number of potential interactions among privileged programs to the minimum for correct operation, so that unintentional, unwanted, or improper uses of privilege are less likely to occur. Thus, if a question arises related to misuse of a privilege, the number of programs that must be audited is minimised. Put another way, if a mechanism can provide 'firewalls', the principle of least privilege provides a rationale for where to install the firewalls. The military security rule of 'need-to-know' is an example of this principle." [12]

Reduce number of users with excessive privileges – AKA least privilege

Now the textbook definition is out of the way we can put this into practical terms. In other words, if your job function involves checking emails, surfing the internet, and running standard applications, then your user account should not be granted administrative rights to your endpoint.

Removing administrative rights from end users is a vital step in improving security by ensuring that endpoints cannot easily be compromised. Preventing unknown processes from running with administrative rights limits the damage that can be done should an

---

11   Department of Defense Trusted Computer System Evaluation Criteria (Orange Book) at http://zedz.net/rainbow/5200.28-STD.html.
12   Department of Defense Trusted Computer System Evaluation Criteria (Orange Book) at http://zedz.net/rainbow/5200.28-STD.html.

endpoint be compromised by malware, as well as reducing the risk of data loss, misconfiguration and insider threats.

In a nutshell, a standard user does not have any administrative rights to the local system, and as such is not able to change critical settings that might affect system stability, security, or other users on the same machine. On the other hand, if you grant a user administrative rights, a piece of malware that is accidently downloaded from the internet has the ability to make system-wide changes and access the same information as your high-privileged administrator account.

Endpoint least privilege is not rocket science

Least privilege security may sound complicated; however, in reality, it is simple - privileges can be assigned to user accounts through the built-in security groups, providing system administrators with an easy way to restrict privileges for the majority of users. While this is not perfect, it is a reasonable trade-off between security and usability.

Although this book focuses on the activities at the endpoint and its security, it is important to consider the broader principle of least privilege and think about how this applies to data access, databases and all aspects of digital and physical security.

Here are my top tips:

- Get the basics right and do not use shared accounts – make sure that your employees and customers are uniquely identified
- Minimise or eliminate all guest and anonymous accounts
- Verify your password policy for best practices regarding complexity, length, and expiration. Make sure that your service account passwords meet these requirements as well

SECURITY FOUNDATIONS

- Privileges should be based on a user's needs, rather than a standard template. Generally this is done with physical security but we often fail to apply the same principles in the digital world

2.2. Application control (AKA whitelisting)

Application whitelisting provides a greater level of control over the software environment. Downloading and running unapproved software is one of the most common ways that devices are compromised. Whereas traditional antivirus technologies laboriously scan every file on the endpoint looking for known bad files/malicious content/threat, whitelisting takes a very different approach and blocks everything except those applications known to be trusted.

2.3. Use of standard, secure system configurations

If every system has a standardised configuration, which is known to be secure, managing these systems and protecting them will be far easier. Define and apply a secure baseline configuration to all devices, and ensure they are updated with the necessary security patches. Ensuring the configuration is continually managed will avoid a security "decay" as new vulnerabilities are reported. If not, attackers will find opportunities to exploit both network-accessible services and client software.

2.4. Patch application and system software

It is vitally important that the operating system and line of business are kept up to date with the latest patches and hotfixes. As I mentioned earlier, one statistic that puts this into context is that 99.9% of vulnerabilities were compromised a year after CVE published![13]

Operating system hotfixes and updates can be managed using Microsoft's Windows Server Update Services (WSUS) or System Centre Configuration Manager (SCCM). A simple example here is that migrating to Windows 8/10 is beneficial in that one of the most commonly exploited applications, Adobe Flash Player, is integrated into Internet Explorer 11 and updated automatically via Windows Update.

Third-party applications often have their own automated patching mechanisms, but some require users to manually install updates and provide consent using an administrative account, forcing IT to choose between removing administrative rights and allowing users to update applications as needed.

2.5. Defence in depth still works – don't just take my word for it

Defence in depth (DiD) is a term coined for a proven military strategy where multiple defences frustrate the enemy and prevent the attack. In the event that one of the security layers is compromised, other layers still provide the necessary protection for the system. Evidence has shown that to combat increasingly complex threats, a layered approach that prioritises high impact and proactive solutions is the best defence.

---

13 http://www.verizonenterprise.com/uk/DBIR/2015/

The four-security foundations discussed in the previous section are recommendations of key industry bodies and when applied together, they offer a substantiated framework for building your DiD strategy.

The Council on Cyber Security states in its 'Critical Security Controls for Effective Cyber Defence' report that a cyber defence system must be based around several "critical tenets" that create a DiD approach.

Established in 2013 as an independent, expert, not-for-profit organisation with a global scope, the Council on Cyber Security is committed to the security of an open internet. The top five recommendations of its 20 Critical Controls, named as "five quick wins", echo findings from the Australian DoD and the UK government, which have also propounded the benefits of a DiD strategy.

By placing the above four strategies at the heart of DiD it is possible to create a balanced, layered approach. Other bodies such as CESG, NIST, CPNI echo the above methods.

Tests have shown the security controls (when implemented together) mitigate 85% of targeted cyber attacks. These recommendations are based on the Australian Skills Directorate's analysis of reported security incidents and vulnerabilities detected by ASD in testing the security of Australian government networks.[14]

---

14   http://www.asd.gov.au/infosec/mitigationstrategies.htm

The removal of administrative rights alone—as recommended by GCHQ (CESG)—mitigates 85% of Critical Microsoft vulnerabilities and 99% of IE vulnerabilities*.[15]

---

15 Microsoft Vulnerabilities Report 2015 http://learn.avecto.com/2015-microsoft-vulnerabilities-report

2.6. Summary: A word of caution – there is no silver bullet!

When it comes to cyber security there is no silver bullet! A layered strategy, combining proactive and reactive measures is needed to properly track, trap and overcome modern cyber attacks.

The four strategies outlined here must be applied fully across 100% of your endpoints (desktops and servers). It only takes one user running with an admin account to be the launch pad into your network.

Get the basic foundations right and the rest becomes much easier.

In the following chapters, I'll show you how.

CHAPTER 3
Good advice is hard to follow

3.1.	100% security or 100% freedom? That is the question	25
3.2.	Why is 100% freedom a challenge?	27
3.3.	Why is 100% security a challenge?	29
3.4.	Operating costs – you cannot win!	33
3.5.	Perception becomes reality	35
3.6.	Summary: User experience is king	37

Having read the previous chapters you may be thinking "I know all this" and if you are, that's a good start. However, ask yourself if you are 100% certain you have applied these principles across 100% of your environment? In my experience most organisations haven't, but the question is why? In this chapter I will explore why organisations often fail to follow the above advice.

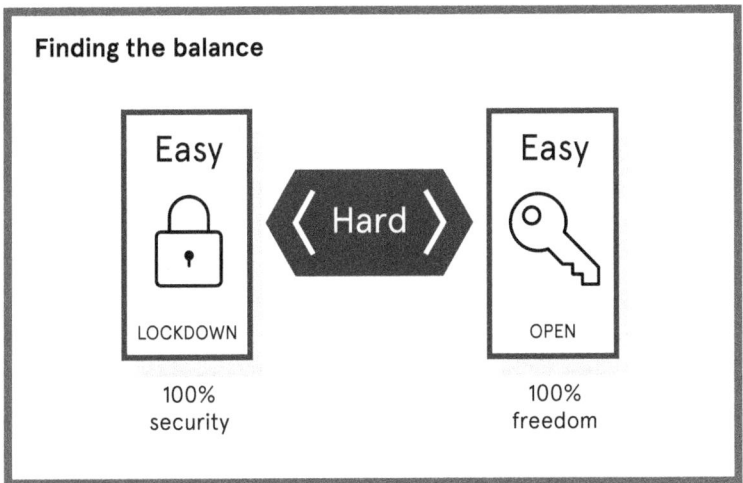

3.1. 100% security or 100% freedom? That is the question

All organisations are faced with a seemingly impossible compromise: your users require flexibility to do their jobs, as well as protection from external and internal attackers and the knowledge that they have a compliant environment in which to work.

 100% freedom is easy! Being 100% secure is easy if you are happy that your users cannot do anything! Liken it to encasing your endpoints in a concrete box – yes they are secure, but the user experience is non existent!

Providing flexibility more often than not means you are faced with giving users too much access to systems, applications and data. Yet to protect the endpoint, you will be required to remove those same elevated privileges that allow them to be productive. How can you reach a compromise?

Constant vigilance is needed to protect your organisation from the ever-shifting attack vectors. If you grant full administrative rights it punches a huge hole in your security posture that is tantamount to professional negligence. But if you lock your users down to a standard user account, the desktops become increasingly difficult to manage. This is because the users require more support and you severely impact their productivity. The issue is compounded by the fact that all corporate IP (Intellectual Property) is stored on or accessed through the endpoint.

Giving users 100% freedom is easy, give them administrative rights and allow them to do what they want, where they want and how they want! They are free but your secure posture is none existent!

Either approach has its downsides, and both come with increased costs and risks. The goal should be providing the right set of privileges and security to meet your organisational and user roles and requirements.

"Companies will struggle to balance security with user productivity especially with the ever increasing tech savviness of Gen Y employees, who expect the same freedoms in work that they have outside of it."

3.2. Why is 100% freedom a challenge?

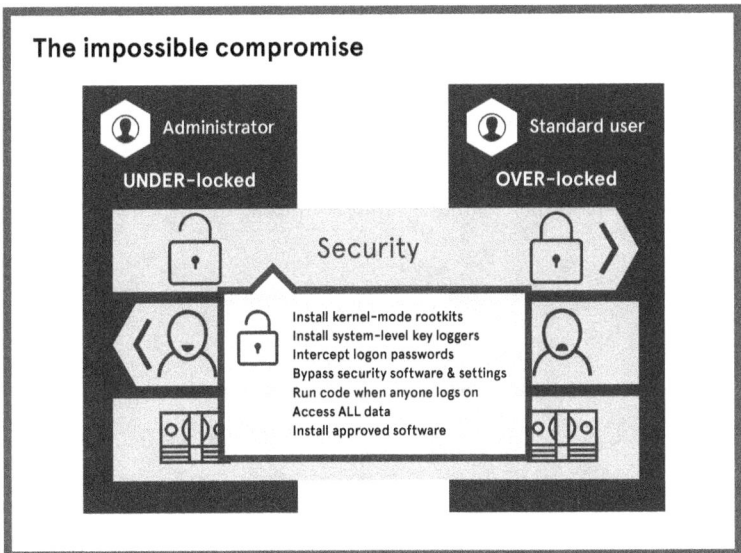

Managing an IT environment is a tough job! I know because I have done it. The board expects the IT department to keep the company's data safe from hackers and unauthorised access, whilst users and middle management often have other ideas about what constitutes good security, preferring to circumvent security policy or have themselves exempted, without a valid business reason. Sometimes, however, complaints about security are justified due to poor design or execution.

The administrator account provides an open and flawed security stance; users and malware potentially have complete access to the system. It is often considered that a single machine running with administrative rights is not a risk to other devices connected to the same network. However, this is not the case. If one device becomes infected with malware, it can pivot the network to launch attacks against other devices, including servers and network hardware. At worst this will bring entire networks to a halt or impede system performance.

Common attacks include:

- Scanning the network for vulnerabilities
- Exploiting pass the hash attacks
- Credential theft for other services running on the network

"If the user has an admin account ALL endpoint protection systems can be disabled one way or another! An admin account is like a bucket full of holes"

In a survey conducted by Ponemon in 2014, 55%[14] of IT professionals admitted to having no visibility of employee behaviour, application access and software downloads and 40% said the percentage of users with administrative rights is increasing year-on-year. This is creating a major security vulnerability and yet often, organisations are not aware of how to solve this issue.

If security gets in the way of a user's ability to do his/her job then it will be weakened or disabled. While such actions may be acceptable as part of the troubleshooting process, configuration changes frequently remain permanent. Administrative rights are often seen as a status symbol to users, especially IT and senior management, they may be reluctant to give them up. If endpoint security is not implemented correctly and users educated effectively, it will most likely start a mutiny!

---

14   https://www.avecto.com/news-and-events/press-releases/study-finds-52-percent-of-enterprises-defenseless-against-cyber-attacks

3.3. Why is 100% security a challenge?

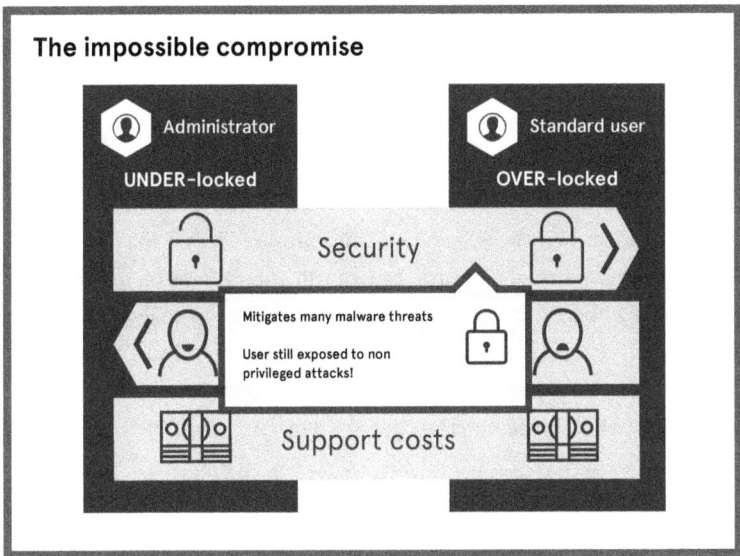

On the other side, the standard user account is the most secure account Microsoft can provide and mitigates the risk of 85% of the critical security vulnerabilities identified in 2015 – with the number of vulnerabilities up 52% year-on-year.

Even back in 2011, Gartner analyst Neil MacDonald stated that removing administrative rights is "the single most important way to improve endpoint security." [15]

Initially it may look like the standard user account has all the answers to our problems, but unfortunately, it does not. The user is still exposed to user data level attacks, such as "ransomware" based exploits. There is a whole host of malware that can run in the context of the standard user and compromise data within their profile. The malware's aim is two-fold; 1) access and steal as much data as possible and 2) proliferate across the network to find a system running with administrative rights, administrative rights in order to embed deeper and cause further damage.

In the example of CryptoLocker, malware infected 600,000 systems and earned its creators more than $1m, with the aim of encrypting all data the user has access to including network shares. Its payloads can be delivered by a wide range of attack sources – websites, documents and fake updates.

---

15 http://blogs.gartner.com/neil_macdonald/2011/08/23/the-single-most-important-way-to-improve-endpoint-security/

Why are administrative rights tolerated?

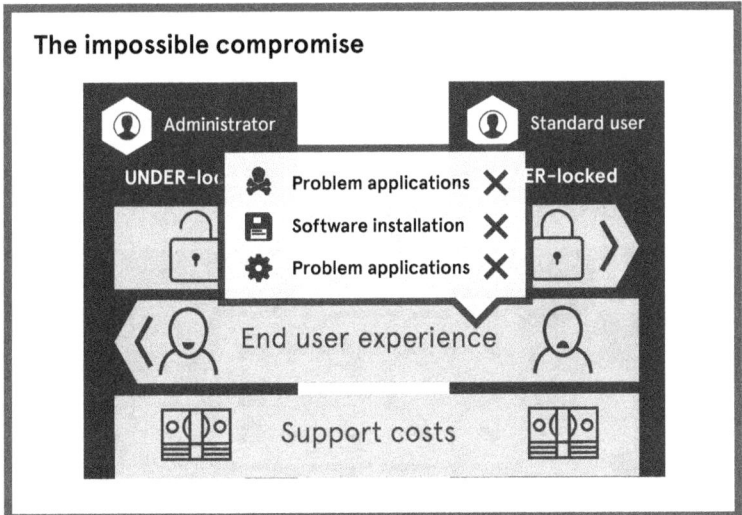

Just removing administrative rights from all users creates challenges in its own right. If a user does not have access to an elevated account, there are hundreds of operating system functions and thousands of applications that will simply not run - Windows 7 alone has over 300 OS functions that require administrative rights to run. The situation is made worse by the fact that IT departments have traditionally relied on users to install approved software and fix problems as directed by the help desk or without any instruction at all. This requires that users have administrative access to systems.

This self-service approach is common, especially in small and medium-sized enterprises, where support staff may not have the necessary skills to help users who do not have full access to their endpoints.

One huge problem you will run into is application compatibility; often caused by developers assuming end users will be logging in with administrator privileges. This results in software that requires administrative rights to work correctly.

Application compatibility problems with least privilege security include; programs failing to launch, not retaining user settings and error messages appearing, all of which inconvenience the end user.

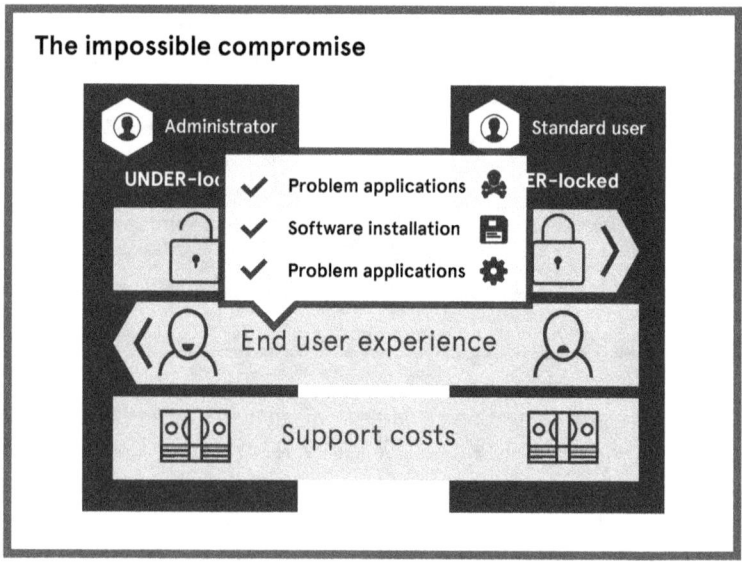

As we've seen, the alternative is that users are given an admin account which then allows them to install any application, run any application and change any setting. This is simply too much power and can lead to issues created by the user. In addition, malware will run in the context of the logged in user and will have access to exactly the same resources as the user.

Non-administrative installations

It has become common for software to be packaged without the need for administrative rights to install. This creates the problem of unauthorised and unlicensed software being introduced. Alternatively, many applications are built in a portable format, meaning that no installation is required, and administrative rights are not needed to run the software. Users can copy the executable file to their endpoint and run the application.

Pertinent examples include Google Chrome, Firefox and other third party browsers. This makes it possible to run applications not sanctioned in corporate environments. Even apps installed to the user's profile can introduce issues and result is data loss.

 Research by Microsoft in 2013 found that 57% of workers install personal software on corporate machines.

3.4. Operating costs – you cannot win!

Finally, neither of the above scenarios minimise the costs of managing your endpoints. Indeed, both have the capacity to increase help desk calls.

With administrative rights, the user may have created issues on the endpoint due to too much access by installing an incompatible application or changing a setting that has implications across your build beyond their knowledge. Imagine the impact from stopping critical system processes from an elevated Task Manager.

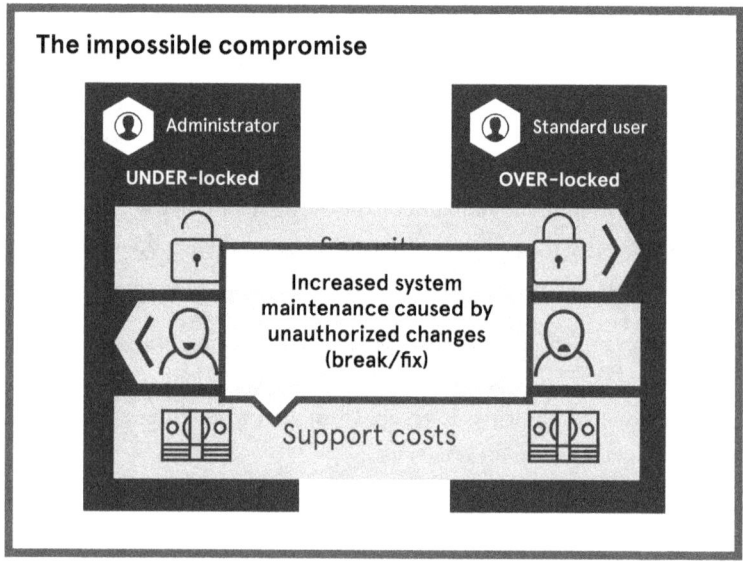

With standard accounts, users are so restricted that they need help performing even simple tasks and have to call the helpdesk to make the most minor of changes. This can mean a physical trip to the desktop in some cases or it can mean a wait of up to six weeks if the app they need has to be packaged and deployed via existing application management systems and processes.

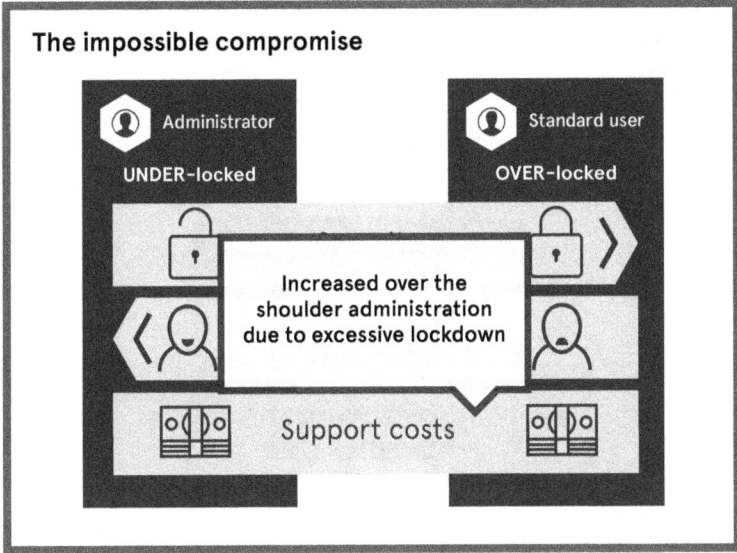

3.5. Perception becomes reality

Due to the complexities involved in the above compromises, there are misconceptions about the effectiveness of security strategies. In a survey of 500+ IT and IT security professionals by Ponemon,[16] a hierarchy of perceived effectiveness was revealed. The table below highlights the tools and technologies organisations ranked in order of importance, which is completely contradicted by the analysis and recommendations of experts such as the Cyber Security Council in association with SANS, GCHQ, CESG, NIST, and the Australian Department of Defence.

---

16   http://www.ponemon.org/local/upload/file/Cyber%20Strategies%20for%20Endpoint%20Defense%20Final1.pdf

THE ENDPOINT SECURITY PARADOX

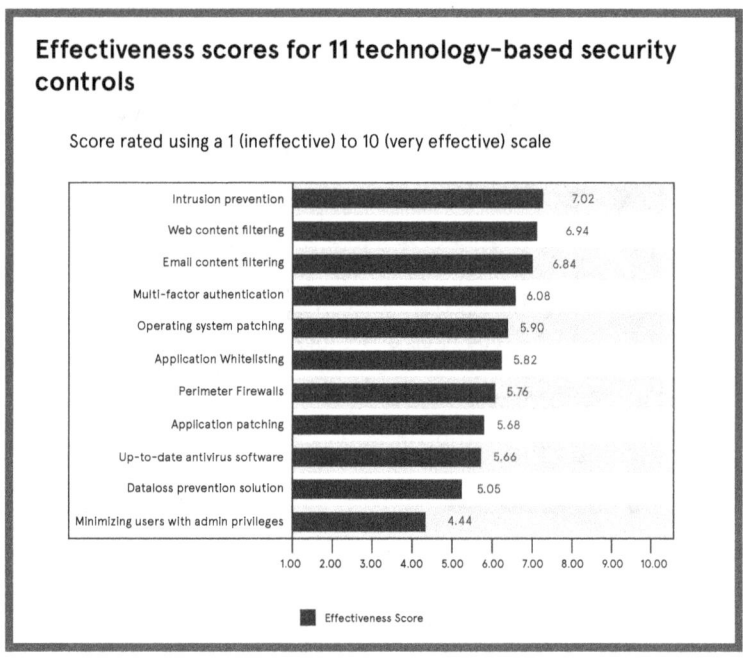

Looking at the above table, the top three technologies are essentially reactive "blacklisting" technologies based on detection. Reactive technologies simply do not work but are often implemented because they are understood and perceived to be easier to rollout. For example, if a "black box" can be implemented which magically stops the threats, this will be perceived as easier, especially if it does not touch the end user.

The same report found that 55% of IT professionals do not have visibility over their endpoints and as a result try to avoid implementing technology that touches the end user. However, this puts them at extreme risk.

3.6. Summary: User experience is king

Navigating the polarised opposites of security and freedom is not easy; this is further compounded when IT departments are under pressure to bring new systems to market that will provide their organisations with a competitive edge.

So many times, I have seen security become an afterthought, rather than being an integral part of a design from the outset. Good security design is not always visible and thus not well understood by the c-suite, who pile on the pressure to release systems or improve user freedom.

Poorly implemented security will come to the forefront when, not if, a breach occurs. The pressure applied to release a system will quickly be forgotten about! To make matters worse, many IT professionals have a limited understanding of security. This lack of understanding often comes from the perception of security not being very "sexy", or worse, an unwanted headache.

There is a risk that endpoint security may reduce your ability to respond to ever-changing business needs. When least privilege security inhibits flexibility or the speed at which IT can respond, it will result in a failed project. So, where security is not an absolute necessity, it is regularly omitted for an easy life.

Securing IT systems to provide business continuity must be balanced with the ability to innovate. Organisations that move slowly will lose out to the competition, as IT systems play a key role in an organisation's agility. However, this is not an excuse for poor security design.

The above examples serve to demonstrate why the key security principles outlined in the previous chapters are not adopted in full.

Build security into a system from the outset, it should be part of your design requirements and not an after thought, that's the only way it will be a success.

GOOD ADVICE IS HARD TO FOLLOW 39

CHAPTER 4

Why typical tools fall short

4.1.	Least privilege – typical tools and tech	41
4.2.	Application whitelisting – typical tools and tech	78
4.3.	Standard secure configurations – typical tools and tech	90
4.4.	Patching – typical tools and tech	93

It is clear from the proceeding chapters what should be done to achieve robust security and the compromises that exist. Yet the question remains; why do the typical tools and technologies available to an organisation fail to allow them to realise the perfect balance between security and freedom? In this chapter, I will look at why organisations and IT professionals have been unable to balance freedom and security with the abundance of tech that exists today.

The sections in this chapter align to the security foundations discussed in chapter 2. I have used or managed teams that have tried to strike a balance using the tools discussed in this chapter. In theory, it is probably achievable with a combination of all the tools below and an infinite amount of time. However, we live in the real world and therefore I will explain what can be achieved and what issues you will come across with each approach.

This chapter focuses on Microsoft technologies due to their pervasiveness, broadly speaking the pros and cons discussed here applied to third party tooling also. I have also focused on the technologies I have seen more commonly used.

4.1. Least privilege – typical tools and tech

Research from the Australian Department of Defence and Cyber Security Council recommends the restriction of administrative rights to operating systems and applications based on user duties. Analysis of Microsoft's security patches shows that removing administrative rights mitigates over 85% of critical security vulnerabilities and is a crucial component for ensuring that other security solutions cannot be tampered with.[1]

If least privilege offers so much, why do so few implement it?

Without controls in place to ensure that users can still function effectively in their day-to-day roles, productivity can suffer. The IT helpdesk can also experience a surge in cases when administrative rights are removed, if users find themselves unable to access applications they need.

Users will often reject least privilege accounts, insisting that "I'll be careful" or "I know what I'm doing". Again, this often comes back to an admin account being a status symbol. The basis for this rejection is often centred around usability. When users undertake risky activities,

---

1 http://learn.avecto.com/2015-microsoft-vulnerabilities-report

such as browsing the internet (computer expert or not), it is impossible to be sure that malevolent software will not be accidently launched through malicious code embedded in web pages. These are designed to launch silently without the user's knowledge, or exploit an unpatched vulnerability in the operating system. Users are the weakest link, increasingly being targeted by the attackers. Recent examples include targeted attacks which pray on the personal assistants of the c-level, to garner information used to find routes into an organisation.

Antivirus software can provide a degree of protection but many exploits cannot be detected, even by the best programs (detection does not work!). Users often put too much faith in antivirus software, believing it will protect them from all evil. Browsing the internet is just one example of a risky activity. Malware can find its way into systems through removable media, CDs, and email, and then propagate throughout a network, causing untold amounts of damage and lost productivity.

Least privilege security is often applied to servers as a matter of course, but the idea of desktop security is regularly limited to the concept of antivirus software and possibly a personal firewall. The benefits that least privilege brings to servers is actually more important on desktops! The reason being the diversity of the locations, content and systems accessed.

In short, implementing least privilege on a Windows operating system stifles the user experience. Unless the people in your environment are classic task-based workers, doing the same job everyday (i.e. call centre staff, Point of Sales (PoS) terminals) you will struggle to make this work.

WHAT DOES WINDOWS OFFER ON ITS OWN?

Windows NT (released in 1993) introduced the ability to log into Windows with a set of system privileges. Privileges range from the ability to change the system time to backing up data. To ease setup, Windows provides a set of built-in groups with pre-assigned privileges, rather than assigning these to individuals. Users are then added to groups, to form role-based access controls.

For a detailed description of the default local groups applying to Windows, and the associated default user rights see Appendix 1.

The default groups are:

- Administrators
- Backup Operators
- Cryptographic Operators
- Distributed COM Users
- Guests
- IIS_IUSRS
- Network Configuration Operators
- Performance Log Users
- Performance Monitor Users
- Power Users
- Remote Desktop Users
- Replicator
- Users
- Offer Remote Assistance Helpers

THE ENDPOINT SECURITY PARADOX

> **Definition:**
> - **Privileges** differ from permissions in that they give users the ability to perform an action
> - **Permissions** allow access to an object such as a file or registry key

Typically, the most used built-in groups are Users and Administrators. If you're assigned to the Administrators group, you can perform almost any task that is not specially protected by the operating system.

Conversely, if you are assigned to the Users group, you can run installed programs and change settings that are not system wide. However, you do not have the privileges to install software to the *Program Files* directory, or modify protected areas of the *registry* or *Windows* directory.

Up until Windows Vista, the *Power Users* were often used to attempt to restrict privileges. This group is essentially an administrator with a few less privileges. Microsoft depreciated this group as it was very easy for Power Users to escalate to full administrative rights.

WHAT'S NEW IN 10?

Many organisations have been waiting for the rollout of Windows 10 to see if it will solve their problems. Windows 10 brings with it Microsoft Passport in conjunction with a new security feature called Virtual Secure Mode (VSM), which protects credentials from Pass-the-Hash (PtH) attacks – a technique used by hackers to move laterally across networks by replaying stolen credentials.

It also aims to replace passwords by making two-factor authentication simpler to deploy.

Microsoft Passport utilises a unique asymmetrical key pair that Windows 10 can generate itself, and store securely with the help of a hardware Trusted Platform Module (TPM). While there will be the option to use keys generated by a PKI, Passport's key-based authentication option will significantly lower the barrier to adoption, and could prove to be more secure than PKI.

Windows 10 will also include Windows Hello, a new feature which for the first time includes the middleware required to make fingerprint readers, iris scanners, and facial recognition hardware work without the need to install anything more than the driver for the device.

Windows Hello bakes all the required software into the OS, and provides an integrated user experience for quick and natural logon without a password.

Summary

Although there are many new security features in Windows 10, there are no fundamental changes to the principles of the NT security model and the 'all or nothing' approach of administrator credentials vs. standard user rights. The features discussed here will protect against Pass the Hash attacks and provide better authentication support, which are welcome additions but will not help with achieving the impossible compromise.

In addition, the technology requires the latest hardware to ensure it will fully function and not impact performance, meaning it will take many years for organisations to migrate to Windows 10. I have listed a number of key points below:

What are the benefits?
- Stops PTH / Mimikatz credential theft
- Tokens / hashes cannot be 'replayed'
- Stops domain creds being used on other devices
- Protects LSASS even on compromised endpoints

What does it require?
- Windows 10 Enterprise x64 with Hyper-V enabled
- UEFI SecureBoot / TPM enabled hardware
- Machine Certificate (automatic in Svr 2016, manual in Svr 2012)

What are the weaknesses?
- Only protects domain credentials, not local or live accounts
- Doesn't protect the Windows Credential Store
- May break 3rd party security providers / authentication providers
- Doesn't prevent exploitation of privileged accounts

USER ACCOUNT CONTROL (UAC) – THE BLACK OR WHITE APPROACH

As discussed earlier, limitations in Windows prevents standard users from performing many common everyday tasks. Microsoft recognised that if running as a standard user requires extra steps, it is likely users will continue to run with administrative rights. User Account Control (UAC), introduced in Windows Vista, is a collection of technologies designed to make it more convenient for users and system admins to run with standard user privileges (most of the time).

User Account Control attempts to automatically determine if a process requires administrative rights and elevate once consent has been given by the user (Admin Approval Mode). This workflow helps ensure that there is a balance between security and freedom. This considerably reduces the risks involved in running with an administrative account. Additionally, it helps programmers develop applications that work without administrative rights.

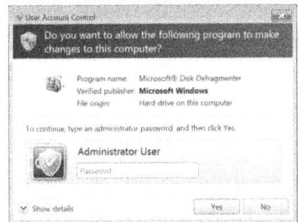

TECHNICAL DEEP DIVE

KEY CONCEPTS

To fully understand the benefits and drawbacks to UAC, it's important to discuss the key concepts on which it is built. The descriptions provided below assume UAC is enabled.

Access tokens

An access token is an object encapsulating the security identity of a process or thread. And it's used to make security decisions. Windows employs the access token when a process or thread tries to interact with objects that have security descriptors (securable objects). The result of this access check evaluation is an indication of whether any access is allowed and, if so, what operations (read, write/modify, etc.) the calling application is allowed to perform.

An access token is generated by the logon service when a user logs on to the system and the credentials provided by the user are authenticated against the authentication database. The authentication database contains credential information required to construct the initial token for the logon session, including its user id, primary group id, all other groups of which it is part of, and other information. The token is attached to the initial process created in the user session and inherited by subsequent processes created by the initial process.

WHY TYPICAL TOOLS FALL SHORT

Standard user access token

When a standard user logs into Windows (Vista and above), Explorer is launched with the standard user's access token. However, when the user wants to elevate an application, they will be prompted to enter alternative credentials to start the process with a user account that has administrative rights. There is no split or filtered token. Therefore, the elevated process is running with a different access token than that of the standard user who logged in and started the desktop session, much the same as in Windows XP when the Run As administrator option is used.

Due to the fact that the elevated process will run in the context of another user account with a different security access token, you should bear in mind that when elevating a process to run with Administrative rights, the elevated process may not have access to the same local and remote resources as the standard user. This illustrates one good reason why using secondary administrative accounts often falls short.

Protected administrator accounts (filtered tokens)

UAC introduced Protected Administrator (PA) accounts to reduce the risks associated with logging on as an administrator. They work by issuing a filtered security access token that runs with standard user privileges until the user gives consent for a process to run with full administrative rights. Essentially the user is granted two tokens - one with administrative rights and one without.

When a Protected Administrator logs on, Explorer is launched with a filtered version of the user's access token. This filtered access token removes all administrative rights and renders it effectively the same as an access token issued to a standard user. Any processes the user launches are also run with the filtered token, unless a request for elevation is made and the user gives consent. In Windows 7, Microsoft configured UAC to auto-elevation for certain Windows binaries.

As Admin Approval Mode runs elevated processes with the same user account and security access token as the user who logged in and started the desktop session, the default configuration is to provide consent for elevation by simply clicking continue. Alternatively, protected administrators can be forced to re-enter their credentials. This can be useful to force users to stop and think for a moment about what they're doing, rather than blindly clicking in a consent elevation prompt. Running an application in the same security context mitigates the issues highlighted with the "run as" approach.

Windows Integrity Levels

Windows Integrity Levels and User Interface Privilege Isolation were introduced to help prevent malicious processes (that run using the filtered access token of a Protected Administrator) injecting code into other processes that have been elevated to run under the same Protected Administrator account with an unfiltered administrative token. The standard Windows security model prevents this when processes run using different user accounts, but as Protected Administrators have what is sometimes referred to as a split token, when they give a process consent to run with full administrative rights, it does so using the same user account.

Windows Integrity Levels assign a level of trust to all objects and processes to prevent those with a low level of trust from accessing objects and processes with a higher level of integrity. Even if you decide to disable UAC it still works. Processes running with lower integrity cannot perform the following actions on processes running with a higher integrity:

1. Inject dynamic link libraries (DLLs)
2. Perform Windows handle validation
3. Monitor a process with journal hooks
4. Use SendMessage or PostMessage functions
5. Attach to a process using thread hooks

Elevation prompts

User Account Control attempts to automate the process of elevating privileges by providing two different types of elevation prompts, depending on whether the user is running as a standard user or a Protected Administrator. Auto-elevation means users do not usually have to decide which processes should run with administrative rights. In addition, it removes the need to right-click on an executable and select Run as administrator from the context menu to elevate a program.

Consent prompts

With the default configuration of Vista and Windows 7, when a user is running with a protected administrator account in Admin Approval Mode, if a process is elevated, a consent prompt is presented. This requires the user to either grant or deny permission for the process to run with administrative rights by clicking Continue or Cancel.

Credential prompts

Sometimes referred to as Over the Shoulder (OTS) prompts, when a user is running as a standard user, they are required to enter the credentials of an administrative account to launch a process with elevated privileges. Prompts may be colour-coded to give the user visual clues as to whether the application is potentially a risk i.e. it has not been digitally signed.

Both the Consent Prompts and Credentials Prompts are displayed on a Secure Desktop (by default). This helps protect the elevation prompt from being attacked by malware as only Windows processes can access the secure desktop, thus helping to protect the privilege credentials.

Filesystem & registry virtualisation

UAC's filesystem and registry virtualisation helps legacy applications run as a standard user by automatically redirecting read and write operations to protected areas of the filesystem and registry (e.g. %ProgramFiles%, %ProgramData%, and %SystemRoot%). These are redirected to a per-user virtual store. This feature does not apply to 64-bit apps, services and Kernel-mode processes, such as drivers.

Pros

- Merges the physical with the virtualised location to present a consist view
- Deleting virtualised files from within applications is supported
- Offers basic file and registry redirection

Cons

- Does not support multiple users who log onto the system, as application files are redirected to the users profile and thus cannot be accessed by other users
- Virtualisation only works for a handful of folders and registry keys. It doesn't cover other 'admin' APIs, which if called from a non-admin app will cause the app to crash. The only way to solve this is to give the user administrative rights, or modify the app to not make those calls
- Does not virtualises executables i.e. if they are copied to the location

Securing Internet Explorer (IE)

Protected Mode in Internet Explorer (the default mode) helps to defend against malware by utilising Windows Integrity Level. IE runs with low integrity, meaning it cannot write/read processes running with a higher-level of integrity. By default, all standard user processes run with medium integrity and all administrator processes run with high. Therefore, malware that may launch from an infected website would not be able to interact with processes outside of IE.

Downsides to UAC

User Account Control cannot ensure complete protection as it is not a security boundary! While it helps to block certain vectors such as shatter attacks, code injection and token hijack, some Windows messages can still be sent from processes with low integrity to those running with high integrity. There have been several well-documented UAC bypasses. Microsoft whitelist some of their own applications so they do not trigger UAC. And when elevating these they can be exploited to launch malware with administrative rights administrative rights without triggering the pop up. Also users who see a UAC prompt that says "Adobe Update" will click ok without thinking. The only way to create a true security boundary that completely isolates running processes is to log on with a standard user account.

Aside from the potential security weakness, the practicalities of UAC must also be considered. When running in Admin Approval Mode, UAC essentially allows the user to do what they want (and when they want) with next to no auditing. Users will simply click "continue" when prompted and could introduce malware into the environment. If users are forced to enter their administrative credentials each time consent is needed they will have a degraded user experience and push back on IT. Additionally, legacy applications that require shared data access among a number of users may fail due to the file and registry virtualisation features.

Although a step in the right direction, UAC is essentially an "all or nothing approach" - it either provides too much freedom or stifles users experience and typically ends up being disabled.

The table below explores more of the practical challenges you may encounter.

Feature	UAC
Control Mechanism	User driven, there is no central control of what can and can't be elevated
Administrative Account Required	Yes (or access to one)
Privileges Assigned	Full administrative rights
Privilege Inheritance	Child processes always inherits the elevated rights of the parent
On Demand	Always available (run as)
Application Types	Executables, installers
Auditing	Very limited
Application Forensics	No
Custom Messaging	No (fixed messages)
User Request	No ability to integrate with central work flows.
Platforms	Windows Vista and above

PAPERING OVER THE CRACKS WITH THE APPLICATION COMPATIBILITY TOOL KIT

Microsoft designed the Windows Application Compatibility Infrastructure to allow the OS to move forward while retaining compatibility with legacy applications. This tool set was originally released with Windows XP to help system administrators and home users solve compatibility problems with applications that were designed to run in earlier versions of the 9x range of Windows.

Compatibility fixes, known as shims, target specific legacy applications, thus allowing them to run in current versions. The advantage of using shims is that rather than maintaining the legacy code in the operating system to ensure that all applications run without modification, the legacy application code is modified by a shim instead of the OS. This makes the OS inherently less complex, more secure and easier to support. When a shim is applied to an application, it intercepts the Win32 API calls from legacy applications and then modifies the call before passing the code to Windows for execution.

Overview of Shim Process

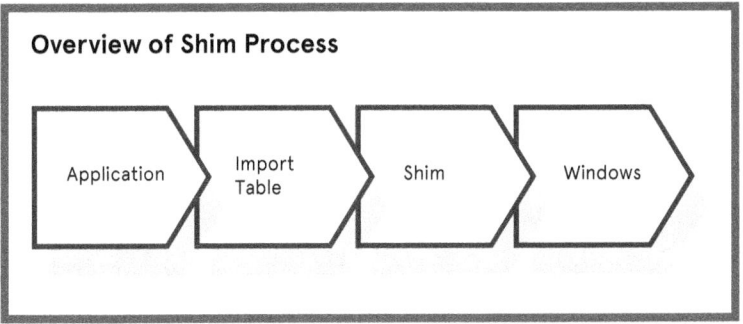

Out of the box compatibility shims

Windows XP, Vista, and Windows 7 all come with a default set of compatibility modes out of the box. These can be used without the need to create custom shims, but as you would expect, they are limited in functionality. Windows Vista and above include the Program Compatibility Assistant that tries to automate the process of applying compatibility fixes to legacy applications by monitoring for known problems. This prompts the user to apply a recommended fix. These fixes include:

- Matching applications against a list of programs with known problems and notifying the user at program start-up
- Errors when launching setup programs
- Failures in install routines
- Failures caused by User Account Control (UAC)
- An install needing to run as an administrator
- A control panel applet requiring administrative rights
- Errors caused because a component is not present in the current version of Windows
- Notifying users about unsigned drivers on 64-bit versions of Windows

Can shims help with least privilege issues?

In short, yes, but it is not straightforward! As discussed, system administrators often grant administrative rights to users or loosen Access Control Lists (ACLs) on files, directories, or registry keys to ensure legacy applications will run, should they need to write to a protected area of the file/registry system.

This increases the attack surface and makes it more likely that systems will be subject to malicious threats, both internal and external. Shims do not require users to hold any additional privileges or modification of security principals and consequently shims are more secure than workarounds, such as relaxing ACLs.

A shim can be used to redirect the requests to a virtualised copy of the protected directory. This can bring with it a new set of problems, especially on shared machines, due to the issues discussed with UAC virtualisation previously.

I would always recommend a shim over weakening ACLs on security principals in an attempt to solve compatibility problems, as this is infinitely more secure. Read and Write operations are the most common reason why legacy programs fail but there are many others and shims provide a solution for a whole host of compatibility issues that weakening ACLs cannot solve.

Windows interprets the modified code presented to it by the shim as code from the application itself. Therefore, application code modified by a shim runs in the same security context as the application and cannot be used to bypass Windows security features.

The downsides to shims

I intimated above that shims could help with least privilege and compatibilities issues, and of course they can. However, I have rarely seen them used successfully, for a whole host of reasons. I have listed these below in order of difficulty.

Developer level application knowledge

The Application Compatibility tool kit requires a developer or system administrator who is familiar with development studios and the application's behaviour to build shims. Once built, an extensive amount of testing must take place in order to ensure the application works as expected. For all but the largest organisations, this functionality remains elusive; many system administrators are not aware of their existence or do not know how to use shims.

I have seen instances of shims being deployed to live environments only to find they break weeks or months down the line, usually because the application has not been fully tested and the end users have triggered the issue by using obscure application features.

Deployment headaches

The shims themselves need to be distributed, either with the application's installer or to the machines affected by the issue. On small networks, where only a handful of legacy applications require shims, it may be feasible to package a custom database with each application. If many applications require shims, a more scalable solution is to maintain a single central custom database and update it on the client machines.

These can be deployed using a Group Policy start-up script. In large organisations I have seen several sets of custom databases deployed to defined categories of users for ease of administration. In addition, you could consider adding a custom database to the OS image. For all of these reasons, shims can be difficult to create, manage and deploy.

Kernel-mode applications

Shims cannot be used to solve compatibility problems with drivers and other software that hooks deep into the operating system. Shims run in user-mode, so the vendor must modify drivers and kernel-mode software if there are compatibility problems.

Vendor support

Essentially, shims mean you are modifying an application's behaviour and therefore run the risk of invalidating any support agreement with the vendor. You should check in advance whether support would be provided if a shim were used to solve a compatibility problem. Of course, in an ideal world, the vendor should fix the problem.

 I have been in situations in the past where vendors have directly refused to look at an issue until the applied shim has been removed, even though it was unlikely to be the cause of the issue.

LEAST VS. LESS PRIVILEGE

Temporary administrative accounts

Windows does not have any built-in mechanism that allows the temporary granting of administrative rights, leaving organisations apprehensive about committing to least privilege. In this section, we will look at a couple of common techniques that I have seen used to grant temporary administrative access.

A primary concern for most organisations is how to support users in break glass situations that require administrator privileges. There are hundreds of examples, from remote workers being at conferences, to research staff needing to test new software. I will cover this in more detail in the section entitled "Supporting least privilege".

Secondary administrative accounts – Good in principle, bad in practice

I often come across organisations that give users two accounts - one with administrative access and one without. The logic behind this is that users will log on with the standard user account and use the 'Run As' administrative function to elevate applications and functions as and when needed. However, in reality, the user generally stays logged in with their administrative account or simply uses this account to add themselves back to the local admins group.

Luckily, there are many things that can be done to prevent this, such as prohibiting the administrative account from accessing email servers and the internet. This often-involves firewall and e-mail server tweaks. You can also configure Group Policy to reset the local user and groups database via the "Restricted Groups GPO or Group Policy preferences". However, with access to a local administrative account it is possible to disable Group Policy within 30 seconds!

Secondary logon service: Windows 2000 introduced the Secondary Logon Service and run as command, which were intended for system administrators in the hope that they'd log on as a standard user and elevate privileges only when required for administrative tasks.

PUNCHING HOLES IN THE OS TO FORCE APPLICATIONS TO RUN

Windows does not provide any built-in means of allowing system administrators to configure an application, task or script to run as the current user (with standard rights), but with an administrative token. Starting applications, tasks and scripts with a secondary administrative account is impractical in most cases and it is often impossible to remedy the issues with the application. In some cases (but not all) privilege problems related to files, folders, and registry keys can sometimes be solved by weakening permissions using Windows Sysinternals tools, such as Process Monitor and Group Policy.

Process Monitor

If an application needs to write to a protected registry key or file but does not have the necessary permissions, you can use Process Monitor from Technet's Sysinternals website to identify the problem files or registry keys. This application will display the files, folders and registry keys an application is trying to access or write to. From here, you will be able to establish any "access denied" issues the application is facing.

Apply the workarounds with Group Policy

The following Group Policy setting - Computer Configuration -> Windows Settings > Security Settings - can be configured to apply changes across multiple computers. I would recommend creating a new GPO to test the settings and apply this to an OU containing a group of test machines prior to any production-wide rollout.

 Please note that any changes you make to permissions on files, folders and registry keys will also be available to other applications running in the context of the logged on users. I have seen malware infect machines because of the above procedure. Essentially, you are opening up security holes in your OS to force an application to work, so caution is always advised.

VIRTUALISING APPLICATIONS

Application Virtualisation is a technology that allows applications to be run on virtualised layers that are isolated from each other and the operating system. This can help to alleviate compatibility issues and problems related to privileges. We are going to focus on App-V in this section, as that is the technology I have most experience of. However, the concepts, advantages and disadvantages are broadly the same across these technologies.

Microsoft App-V

Application Virtualisation technology, is a component of the Microsoft Desktop Optimisation Pack (MDOP), which can be licensed by organisations with Software Assurance. Applications run in dedicated virtualisation layers and there's no need to deploy virtual machines, which saves a lot of time. App-V programs can be streamed from a server on the corporate network or across the internet, as well as being available offline. They can also be managed centrally, so that if an application is updated on an App-V server, those changes are automatically streamed to App-V clients.

App-V works by creating a virtualised bubble for each application using a technology called SystemGuard. Each bubble isolates an application from the host operating system and from other applications. System services (Windows services, COM, OLE, printers, fonts, cut and paste), files (DLLs, .ini files, and so on), and registry keys are all virtualised in separate bubbles. SystemGuard monitors the App-V programs and redirects calls to virtualised resources, such as system services, files, and registry keys. This enables programs to run without actually installing them on the host operating system.

Using this technology on the desktop we can:

- Eliminate conflicts with other applications running on the same host OS
- Allow legacy applications that require administrative rights to run under a standard user account
- Run different versions of the same application on the same host OS
- Update applications on a central server and stream the changes to desktops
- Allow standard users to run applications on demand without the need to elevate to administrative rights
- Stream only the required elements of an application suite
- Enable applications to follow users who work on multiple devices

Using App-V to help with administrative rights

There are no Access Control Lists (ACLs) that prevent a standard user from modifying the application's virtual registry or filesystem within a virtual bubble. This means that most programs will have no privilege issues within an App-V bubble. If an App-V program is allowed to pass through to the host OS to read or write to a file or registry key, ACLs apply to the logged in user as if the application was running locally on the host OS, and therefore could still have issues.

App-V packages can provide a way of enabling user self-service, where users can choose which applications to install and when to install them. This can all be done without administrative rights.

Alternatives to App-V

For completeness, I will briefly mention some alternatives here. VMware's ThinApp system is similar to App-V, but the client is embedded into the sequenced package, Virtual Operating System (VOS), and doesn't require that the client be "installed" like App-V's kernel-mode client does. Citrix XenApp and Symantec SVS Pro also deploy a kernel-based agent like App-V for Application Virtualisation and streaming.

Downsides to Application Virtualisation

Application Virtualisation gives organisations the ability to deploy secure, but at the same time, flexible systems. In truth, I have had some great success with App-V but it's not a panacea. Firstly, you need an MDOP licence. Secondly, you need to create, test and manage the App-V packages. This in itself is not the easiest thing to do, especially if the application needs access to the OS or needs to save data outside the App-V bubble. Although App-V can help in many ways, you will find that it is only viable where the time of creating packages is cost justifiable.

USING VIRTUAL DESKTOP INFRASTRUCTURE (VDI) TO SOLVE PRIVILEGE ISSUES

While it is always best to avoid virtualisation technologies to solve compatibility fixes, in the real world that is not always possible. Virtual Desktop Infrastructure(VDI) provides organisations that do not have the technical resources or time to solve compatibility issues with a fast, if not ideal, solution.

There are many VDI technologies in this space, including some standalone solutions. Windows 7 included XP Mode as a way of solving application compatibility problems. It allows users to run programs in a pre-configured virtual machine, while also running Windows XP. To help manage these machines, MDOP includes technology called Microsoft Enterprise Desktop Virtualization (MED-V).

Typically, you will see VDI deployed and managed via technologies from VMware, such as ESX technology and Hyper-V from Microsoft. All of these technologies provide a way to virtualise and deliver an OS to the user over the network.

The important thing to remember is that these are full OS' and in most cases will be joined or have access to your network. Therefore, you are shifting the problem from the user's local machine into the data centre.

 Clients often tell me that all their users are standard users and they have Application Control applied to their machines, only to find each of their developers has a VDI machine on which they are an admin and can do whatever they like. These machines need to be managed in the same way that any other device would be.

Another common consideration is image persistence. If you are planning on non-persistent images, there are a few things to consider. The non-persistent VDI will be destroyed upon logoff so malware will be eliminated. Therefore, you could argue that the OS would not need the same protection that a fat or persistent image is subject to. However, the enterprise is vulnerable to attacks for the time the user is on the network during their session and this endpoint could be used to gain entry to the network. Another consideration is the user experience that non-persistent images pose: the end-user will have no ability to configure the OS to suit their working requirements. The leads to an inflexible and potentially poor user experience.

SYSTEM CENTRE CONFIGURATION MANAGER (SCCM)

System Center Configuration Manager (SCCM) is a systems-management software product developed by Microsoft for managing large groups of computers running Windows, Windows Embedded, Mac OS X, Linux or UNIX, as well as various mobile operating systems such as Windows Phone, Symbian, iOS and Android. It provides remote control, patch management, software distribution, OS deployment, network access protection, and hardware and software inventory.

There have been many iterations of the solution, adding features such as the ability to manage SCCM configuration by AD site. I typically see software distribution, patch management and inventory management as the most widely used features. However, SCCM also includes technologies like its advance client feature, which is capable of dealing with distributed networks and remote clients that may not always connect back to the same SCCM service.

Downsides to SCCM

I have seen organisations have some great success with SCCM when it comes to OS deployment, patch management and the deployment of sanctioned line of business applications. Where it does less well is in the ability to deal with flexible on-demand installations/changes. What I mean by this is the ability to quickly deploy software or configuration changes, which only a handful of users need. The packaging, testing and deployment overheads are too large to be cost effective. This results in users being given administrative rights to install and make systems changes or changes, or the IT team completes the activity on the user's behalf.

USING SYSTEM IMAGES FOR SOFTWARE DISTRIBUTION

Enterprises will typically utilise imaging technologies, such as Windows Deployment Services or similar, to pre-configure the OS and applications, then deploy them over the network from a dedicated server. Organisations that can afford the necessary infrastructure and have the required skills, can overcome some of the problems associated with deploying software to users running with Least Privilege Security, by leveraging imagining technology.

Many companies choose a combination of imaging and other management systems for maximum flexibility. Typically, there are two approaches to client images - thin and fat:

- **Thin** images contain just the OS and the minimum number of additional components. The rest of the settings are applied and controlled via Group Policy and tools such as SCCM.
- **Fat** images contain the OS and all the required line of business applications. When new applications are required, the image is updated and redeployed.

WHERE DOES GROUP POLICY FIT IN?

One area Group Policy can help with is the installation of software. This is often seen as one of the biggest challenges to implementing least privilege: If admin privileges are removed users have to rely on an administrator or a software distribution system to install or update applications. The Group Policy Software Installation system helps with this challenge as it allows for Group Policy objects to be targeted at the users and computers that require software to be installed. However, its functionality is limited and I would only recommend this for small and medium-sized businesses. For large enterprises, I would suggest using System Centre Configuration manager or another third party software distribution platform instead, as they offer more functionality. I'll discuss this option later.

Deploying software with Group Policy

Group Policy Software Installation requires applications to be packaged in Windows Installer .msi format. This in itself is a problem, as many older applications rely on older setup technologies, which usually end with the .exe file extension and don't contain an .msi file. These types of installers are not supported by GPSI installation. Technically speaking, you have the option of creating a .zap package. However, this involves taking a snapshot of a machine before and after installation. In addition, the logged in user must be an administrator to complete the installation process. In practical terms, unless the application is packaged as an MSI, it's unlikely to be worth the effort.

Startup scripts

When it is not practical to leverage Group Policy Software Installation for software deployment, such as legacy installers, a plausible option is to create a start-up or login script. These can be used to automate the installation routes and are deployable via Group Policy. Start-up scripts will run in the system context and would not need administrative rights (and could introduce potentially dangerous mistakes), whereas login scripts run in the context of the logged in user. One thing to be aware of is these scripts can be complicated to create, test and manage so they don't provide a quick deployment option and will most likely only be used for applications, which many users need. GPSI deployment provides better lifecycle and awareness of the installation state.

Downsides to Group Policy Software installation

In short, Group Policy functionality is limited and will only be useful in the smallest of organisations. In later sections, I will discuss the application of settings using Group Policy.

WHAT ABOUT PRIVILEGED IDENTITY MANAGEMENT (PIM)?

Many businesses, financial institutions and regulated authorities have implemented a Privileged Identity Management (PIM) solution to address regulatory requirements for the monitoring of privileged user activity. These solutions are especially relevant for servers which are controlled by IT / system administrators (sysadmins).

Such solutions are traditionally designed to grant secure access to specific destinations via a password vault. When a sysadmin requests access to a specific server, the vault will grant it by providing a temporary administrative account and then begin recording the session. Access rights will be given for the duration of the session until the task is completed, and the session is closed.

The key benefits of such solutions come from the tight control of login credentials, ensuring the sysadmin never has visibility of the password. This increases the organisation's security defences against unauthorised configuration changes, data compromise and other insider threats.

Additionally, session recording is used to ensure that regulated companies have the tools to meet their audit requirements for the monitoring of privileged activity.

However, session recording alone is inadequate when adhering to many audit requirements, security policies, or indeed, the more advanced internal and external threats that are facing organisations every day.

These solutions, when used in isolation, simply do not provide enough protection. Assuming that sysadmins do not attempt to hide their unauthorised activity, any damage captured in recording has already been done. The challenge for IT teams is to find a solution that enhances and complements their existing vaulting and session recording technology.

By building upon their original investment, organisations can increase their security defences and take a more proactive stance to combat today's advanced threats.

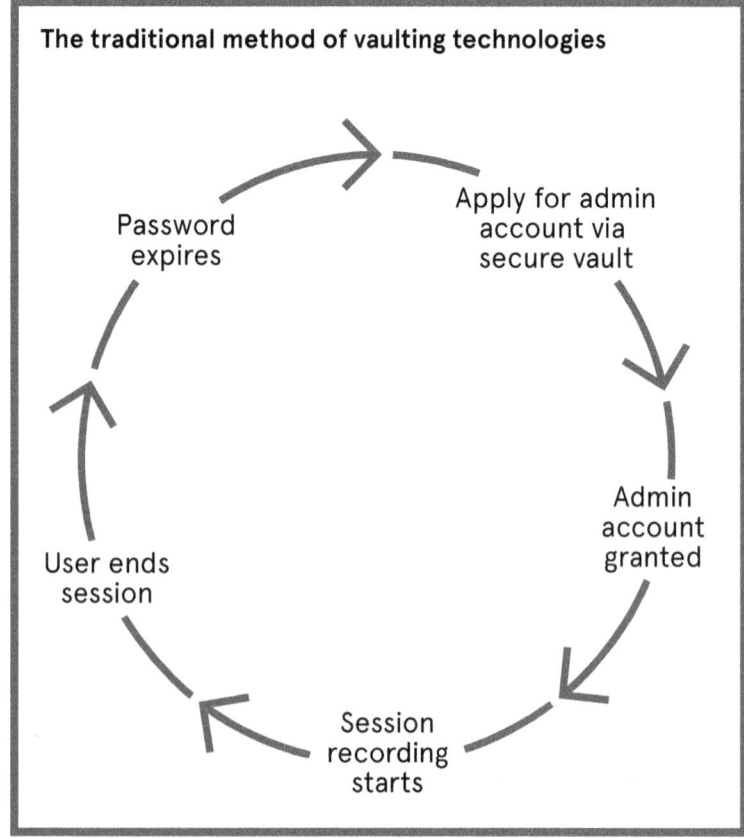

The traditional method of vaulting technologies

"60% all attacks in 2015 were carried out by insiders. 44.5% malicious, 15.5% inadvertent actors."
— IBM Cyber Security Intelligence Index [2]

DOWNSIDES TO PIM

Administrator accounts are issued

While the vault controls and permits server access when required, an administrator account is still issued for the duration of the session. The dangers of administrator privileges have been well-documented, acting as the back door into the heart of the business and its data. Administrator accounts are frequently targeted by hackers and malware, with the potential to be exploited by insiders (whether through deliberate or unintentional misuse). Sysadmins are the most powerful form of user, with full and unrestricted access to perform any task.

Administrator sessions can be left active

Typically, vaults and recording use logon/logoff triggers to identify the beginning and end of a session. It is possible for sysadmins to circumnavigate or bypass the controls by simply 'disconnecting' their session, leaving it running so they can reconnect later.

Session recording is a reactive security measure

Session recording captures the steps taken during the open session in CCTV-style fashion, so that if a breach was to occur, the footage could be examined to establish the cause. The flaw in session recording as a standalone solution can be summarised in the analogy of a bank

2 http://www-01.ibm.com/common/ssi/cgi-bin/ssialias?subtype=WH&infotype=SA&htmlfid=SEW03133USEN&attachment=SEW03133USEN.PDF

robbery: CCTV records the crime, and the perpetrator might later be identified and apprehended from the taped evidence. While acting as a deterrent, the recording does not prevent the crime from happening in the first place. The same applies when dealing with data but unlike a bank robbery, perpetrators can infiltrate a network days, week or months before any damage is done.

The challenge for many organisations is in the storage and management of session recordings, which represent a heavy resource impact both in terms of physical storage and also for employees to review and manually annotate endless hours of footage.

Ask yourself the following questions to help establish if session recording is really the answer:

- Who is looking at these recordings?
- Does the reviewer understand what they are looking at?
- What is INSIDE that script named "UpdateSettings.ps1" that was run? Did they add a local admin account in the script or schedule some additional tasks to run later on?
- Has the horse bolted? Were organisational interests compromised? It's done... damage control starts now.

Removing excess administrative rights is considered to be one of the most essential risk mitigation strategies for organisations and IT departments globally, immediately improving the security posture of any organisation and enabling regulatory compliance.

This is because removing administrative rights from the network significantly reduces the attack surface and potential for security breaches. Nevertheless, this approach has traditionally created challenges in the data centre, causing sysadmins to be overly restricted and prevented from performing their day-to-day roles. I will be discussing how these challenges can be solved in later chapters.

SUPPORTING THE END USER

To this day, Microsoft Windows (Windows 10 included) does not provide a comprehensive solution for the problem of balancing security with user freedom. There are many potential workarounds that organisations have attempted, but historically they have not been able to be properly utilised or they consume too much resource while leaving the organisation open. This ultimately leading to a failed solution. I have discussed the difficultly of balancing security with freedom in the previous sections, so I will now look at the problems from the IT department's perspective. This adds further evidence as to why typical tools fail to deliver in the real world.

Supporting least privilege

IT staff must have a detailed understanding of the following in order to support standard users:

- **Windows security model:** Access control lists (ACLs), NT user rights, Integrity Levels, and User Account Control are all components of the security model, with the exception of Integrity Levels and User Account Control. Many Windows support professionals have a limited understanding of these concepts.
- **Command line or PowerShell:** While GUI-based remote access tools can be useful, they are not always the most efficient way to gather data or run commands on remote computers, especially over slow network connections.
- **Automated software and patch installation:** Technologies such as Group Policy Software Installation, Windows Server Update Services (WSUS), System Centre Configuration Manager, or App-V.
- **Management infrastructure:** Active Directory, Group Policy, or System Centre Configuration Manager.

Without the proper infrastructure in place, IT staff will have to "visit" users' desktops, either physically or through remote access far more often. The points listed above become crucial when supporting standard users, as a managed infrastructure is required.

Often IT professionals simply grant administrative rights to users, as they do not understand how to work with "managed systems", or simply do not have the time or will to investigate the problem. As mentioned above, these rights are often left in place.

Remote support

Support tools such as Remote Desktop have been around for a long time and form part of the help desk's tool set. When users are running with standard user accounts, these tools are critical. The main reason for this is that you can no longer talk a user through a procedure over the phone if it requires administrative access (unless you create an administrative backdoor, although I would not advise it).

Prepare for the worst

I can pretty much guarantee the standard method of connecting to the corporate network will break at some point so provide at least one back up remote connection method. Also, be prepared for GUI-based remote access tools (i.e. Remote Desktop and Remote Assistance) to fail over slow network links. Set up remote access via the command line using WS-Management and PowerShell. These command line tools can save the day and often speed up support. The downside is they require advanced knowledge.

Remote and home based workers

In my experience, remote workers are given administrative rights 95% of the time. I often smile to myself when I go into an organisation and I'm told no one has administrative rights. I then ask how they support remote workers, only to find they, of course, get admin accounts. Remote workers bring with them a whole host of problems; greatest among them is that their devices need to stay up-to-date and distributing new software when required can be a nightmare. The solution? Consider technology, such as System Centre Configuration Manager, which provides the ability to distribute software and patches over slow network connections. In addition, they often need support when connecting to devices and systems at tradeshows and customer sites.

DirectAccess is a good solution for users who are always on the road or in remote locations, but unfortunately it's not widely implemented.

Network Access Protection (NAP) or similar can be used to ensure that returning remote workers are checked for compliance with security policies before allowing them full access to corporate networks.

Supporting peripherals

It's important to establish what and how your organisation will be supporting peripheral equipment. For example, what are laptop users allowed to connect to their endpoints? Create a list of approved devices (such as printers, mobile phones etc). A typical problem most IT teams have is laptop users' purchasing their own home office devices and expecting that support will be provided.

Standard users are limited as to what drivers they can install, which is often the root cause of support issues on peripherals. Standard users can install drivers if:

- The device driver is included in Windows out of the box
- IT have pre-staged in the local driver store (having a standardised list helps here)
- A driver is digitally signed according to the Windows Driver Signing Policy
- A driver signed according to the Windows Driver Signing Policy or by a publisher that is already trusted by the local computer is available and the associated device GUID is listed in the Allow non-administrators to install drivers for these device setup classes policy setting (Windows Vista and later)

SUMMARY - THE PATH OF LEAST RESISTANCE

As you can see, there is a lot to get right. There is always some external pressure applied to IT departments, which results in corners being cut and leads to an increased attack surface. If there was an infinite amount of resource and time the typical tools could be combined to solve the problem. Unfortunately, we all know that is not the case.

4.2. Application whitelisting – typical tools and tech

Removing administrative rights goes a long way to securing user accounts and protecting critical parts of the system from accidental or malicious change. If you have done these things, you should be pleased with yourself (and proud). However, the user and the system are still exposed to applications and malware that can execute from the users profile, such as portable apps, as well as vulnerabilities in trusted line of business applications.

Therefore, we need to configure the build to only allow the execution of trusted applications and block the execution of the unknown. This is achieved with a whitelist and it's crucially important, as modern modular APT (Advanced Persistent Threat) attacks use a myriad of techniques to drop payloads in the attempt to exploit a zero day attack. A recent example of this is operation Russian doll. Here is a high level flow of the exploit:

1. User clicks link to attacker-controlled website
2. HTML/JS launcher page serves Flash exploit
3. Flash exploit triggers CVE-2015-3043, executes shellcode
4. Shellcode downloads and runs executable payload (app control would have prevented)
5. Executable payload exploits local privilege escalation (CVE-2015-1701) to steal System token

Rated by industry analysts, such as SANS, as well as compliance mandates like GCHQ, NIST etc as 'essential', application whitelisting is crucial for preventing malware. A whitelist is a set of programs, scripts, or processes that are trusted and therefore approved to run. It is a good practice to create a whitelist of permitted applications, rather than blocking banned programs using a blacklist. It is impossible to include every malicious application in a blacklist, so it is preferable to attempt to define what is allowed in a whitelist.

Typically, whitelists have been difficult to create and maintain. However, basing the list on trusted locations rather than individual applications ensures the list is easy to maintain. This allows for the effective control of applications by adding known and trusted locations/sources to whitelists, while unknown and untrusted apps are prevented from executing actions that can threaten the system.

 In this section I'll look at the tools available in Windows for Application Control

WINDOWS APPLOCKER

Designed as a replacement for Software Restriction Policy (SRP) and introduced in Windows 7, AppLocker is designed to overcome the shortcomings of SRP. Small and medium enterprises rarely deploy SRP, especially in Windows XP. This is due to problems with launching applications from shortcuts, and because Path Rules are too easy to circumvent in many cases. SRP certificate rules offer limited configuration options and Hash Rules are problematic when applications are upgraded.

AppLocker is more flexible and easier to configure, with the ability to automatically generate rules and apply strong certificate rules based on a variety of different criteria.

Applocker rule types

Path Rules enable you to restrict the execution of programs to a certain directory path. For example, you can allow end users to launch applications only from the Windows Program Files folders. This is safe as long as end users are running with a standard user account. The problem with this rule type is that users often also need to start applications from other locations, for example, from a file server. Depending on the complexity of the environment, it can be time-consuming to keep track of legitimate program folders.

Hash Rules use a cryptographic hash of the executable to identify a legitimate program. The major downside of this rule type is that you have to modify the rule whenever you update the program, because any kind of change to the executable will also alter the hash.

Publisher Rules identify an application based on a digital signature of the application that was issued by the publisher. They are comparable to the Certificates Rules found in the Software Restriction Policies. However, Publisher Rules are more sophisticated. Most new applications have a digital signature that can be used for Publisher Rules. In Vista and Windows 7, you can view this digital signature through the file properties of the executable.

In addition, Publisher Rules have more options than Certificate Rules. They allow you to work with different scopes. You can restrict the execution of a program to the publisher (for example, Microsoft), to the product name (Internet Explorer), to the file name (iexplore.exe), or to the file version (8.0.0.0). Note that the file version does not necessarily correspond with the program version. It is also possible to restrict the rule to a specific version only, to a specific version number and above, or to a specific version number and below. Because AppLocker gets this information from the digital signature of the executable, end users can't circumvent Publisher Rules by just renaming a file.

All three rule types (Path, Hash, and Publisher) can be applied to executables (.exe), to scripts (.ps1, .bat, .cmd, .vbs, .js), to installer files (.msi, .msp), and to system libraries (.dll, .ocx)

Exceptions: All rule types allow you to configure exceptions. An exception can be one of the three rule types, and it can be a different rule type from the rule it belongs to. For instance, you could configure a Path Rule that allows the execution of all apps in the Program Files folder except those of the publisher Microsoft. This would prevent users from launching Internet Explorer, Windows Media Player, etc. Or you could restrict the rule to a certain user or user group. It is also possible to configure 'allow' and 'deny' rules. 'Deny' rules have a higher priority than 'allow' rules.

Downsides to Applocker - administrative rights & user experience

Although Applocker has been used much more than Software Restriction Policies, it has not been widely implemented. This is mainly a result of its manageability and user experience. Crucially, AppLocker does not allow organisations to assign administrative rights to applications rather than users. If applications or operating system functions require administrative rights, organisations using AppLocker would still need to assign them to the user and thus open up systems to abuse. Essentially, it's not hard to bypass AppLocker. I have listed four ways to disable AppLocker below as an admin, none of which require you to be deeply tech savvy:

1. Stop the Application Identity service (AppIDSvc)
2. Right click an executable and choose "Run as Administrator"
3. Create Local AppLocker polices (which would then merge with the GPO settings)
4. Boot into SafeMode

WHY TYPICAL TOOLS FALL SHORT

The table below details other areas of consideration.

Feature	AppLocker
Group Policy	Computer only
Application privileges	No – applications run in the context of the logged on user
Application control	Allow, deny
Application types	Executables, installers, scripts Note: installers will rely on UAC if administrative rights required
Application rules	Path, hash, publisher
Auditing	Yes – basic
Application Forensics	No
Custom Messaging	No
User Request	No
Platforms	AppLocker is available in all editions of Windows Server 2008 R2 and in Windows 7 Ultimate and Windows 7 Enterprise. Windows 7 Professional can be used to create AppLocker rules. However, AppLocker rules cannot be enforced on computers running Windows 7 Professional. Windows 8, Windows Server 2012 and Windows 10

Rule creation can also be a problem. I've spoken to a lot of companies that have an "audit only" policy they use to establish which processes they need to whitelist and from what locations. This brings with it an overhead from two aspects. Firstly, machines have to be moved under the management of audit policies; Secondly, logs need to be interpreted to create the final Applocker policies. As there is no integration between logs and policy, the management overhead is high.

DEVICE GUARD - WINDOWS 10

Device Guard gives organisations the ability to lock down devices in a way that provides advanced malware protection against new and unknown malware variants, as well as Advanced Persistent Threats (APT's). It provides better security against malware and zero days for Windows 10 by blocking anything other than trusted apps (digitally signed applications), the Windows Store, or even your own organisation's applications. Companies can decide what sources Device Guard considers trustworthy and it comes with tools that can make it easy to sign Universal or even Win32 apps that may not have been originally signed by the software vendor.

Device Guard achieves its goals by combining the following components:

- Secure Boot
- Kernel Mode Code Integrity
- User Mode Code Integrity
- Trusted Platform Module (TPM)
- Virtualisation Based Security

Essentially, Device Guard is Application Control (whitelisting) with some advanced features. Any app location other than those explicitly trusted are blocked. Good applications are trusted using digital signatures as a primary method of identification.

The Local Security Authority (LSA) can create a virtual secure mode that prevents hash attacks (e.g. pass the hash) by running outside of the main O/S in a sterile environment. Even if the parent O/S is compromised, this environment is preserved.

The "Kernel mode integrity" component moves the Code Integrity outside of the kernel, and Windows checks to see if a software package has been officially signed by Microsoft (or a trusted publisher). This theoretically prevents rogue/malicious software from running in what Microsoft terms as "user mode code integrity".

The virtualisation/hypervisor-based approach keeps things safe by moving the security feature outside of the main OS, but this is hardware-dependent. When an application is run, Windows determines if the app is trustworthy. By using hardware and virtualisation to isolate this decision-making process outside of Windows, Device Guard remains secure and safe, even if a malicious code gains access to full system privileges.

How Device Guard works

When the device starts it boots using Universal Extensible Firmware Interface (UEFI) Secure Boot, so that boot kits cannot run and so that Windows 10 Enterprise starts before anything else.

After securely starting up the Windows boot components, Windows 10 Enterprise can start the Hyper-V virtualisation-based security services, including Kernel Mode Code Integrity. These services help protect the system core (kernel), privileged drivers, and system defences - like anti-malware solutions - by preventing malware from running early in the boot process, or in kernel after start-up.

Device Guard uses UMCI to make sure that anything that runs in user mode, such as a service, a Universal Windows Platform (UWP) app, or a Classic Windows application, is trusted, allowing only trusted binaries to run.

At the same time that Windows 10 Enterprise starts up, the trusted platform module (TPM) launches. TPM provides an isolated hardware component that helps protect sensitive information, such as user credentials and certificates.

Configuration and deployment

By design, Device Guard features no user interface. Instead, Microsoft has chosen to document the format of the technology to allow third parties (which includes Microsoft's own SCCM team) to develop front-end tools and allow integrations into existing management systems.

Management is achieved through a combination of Group Policy (or an MDM for mobile W10 devices) and PowerShell.

In order to implement the whitelisting of applications, as noted above, they must be signed. This is achieved through a number of routes:

- Using the Windows Store publishing process. All apps that come out of the Microsoft Store are automatically signed with special signatures that can roll-up to their certificate authority (CA) or to your own.
- Using your own digital certificate or public key infrastructure (PKI), ISV's and enterprises can sign their own Classic Windows applications themselves, adding themselves to the trusted list of signers.

- Using a non-Microsoft signing authority. ISV's and enterprises can use a trusted non-Microsoft signing authority to sign all of their own Classic Windows applications.
- Using a Microsoft-provided web service ISV's, enterprises will be able to use a more secure, Microsoft-provided web service to sign their Classic Windows applications.
- Microsoft are also supporting "Catalogue signing", which is a means to support one or more binaries without embedding signatures. This in turn will require applications to be re-packaged. It's the mechanism required for driver packages and can be deployed separately to the actual binaries the catalogue refers to.

Required software and hardware

Hardware certified for use with Windows 8 will be compatible with Device Guard. However, to get support for the hypervisor element you will need Intel's VT-D compatible CPU (i.e. i3 [Latest Gen], i5, i7, Xeon etc.).

The full feature set of Device Guard will also require support by hardware vendors for elements like UFEI boot and TPM etc. Consequently, not every system will be able to leverage all the functionalities - particularly if you are upgrading or re-imaging existing (older) hardware.

An interesting point to note is that Device Guard is only available in the Windows Enterprise version. This is what most large organisations will run, as the Pro version is aimed at SMEs (although the Pro version is the natural upgrade version for Win 7 Pro and Ultimate).

Downsides to Device Guard - target market / limitations

Microsoft says Device Guard's full set of features is aimed largely at very tightly managed fixed-function systems (such as ePOS terminals, kiosk systems and ATMs) with few updates and settings changes and no admin users (or possibly no active users at all). A secondary target for Microsoft is corporate environments thatare "fully managed", meaning that the organisation is working with only known hardware and a known software catalogue (i.e. users only ever run pre-approved applications).

The end user experience is extremely limited, with yet more unintuitive messaging, no user support, and no ability to customise the messaging presented to the end user. The inference from Microsoft is that this will change in future releases.

It is also not compatible with BYOD (Bring Your Own Device) because of the reliance upon hardware features for certain aspects and because it would require the end user to consent to their device being taken over by the organisation.

Finally, not only is the solution difficult to configure due to lack of a user interface, it also requires the system to be rebooted for configuration changes to be applied.

The above design limitations will severely hinder the uptake of devices to fixed function products and situations where users do not interact with devices. I initially hoped that Device Guard would help balance security with freedom in the enterprise, but unfortunately, this is simply not the case. It is too restrictive and the configuration overheads will limit its deployment to fixed environments.

SUMMARY

The biggest drawback to application whitelisting is creating a list of known good applications and ensuring it cannot be circumvented. I have discussed above how easy Applocker is to disable if you have administrative rights or a secondary admin account. This is typically the case for third party solutions.

Additionally, the list of known good applications has traditionally been resource-heavy to create and maintain thereafter. How do you discover all the applications which are trusted? How do you deal with a situation where an end user needs to install an "untrusted" application?

Of course, there are work arounds. To handle exceptions, you need to allow Applocker to run and then you need the application to install with administrative rights and be configured for the user's profile. This isn't easy though and even if you do manage to deploy a secure and workable policy, it must be continually maintained as new applications and requirements are introduced.

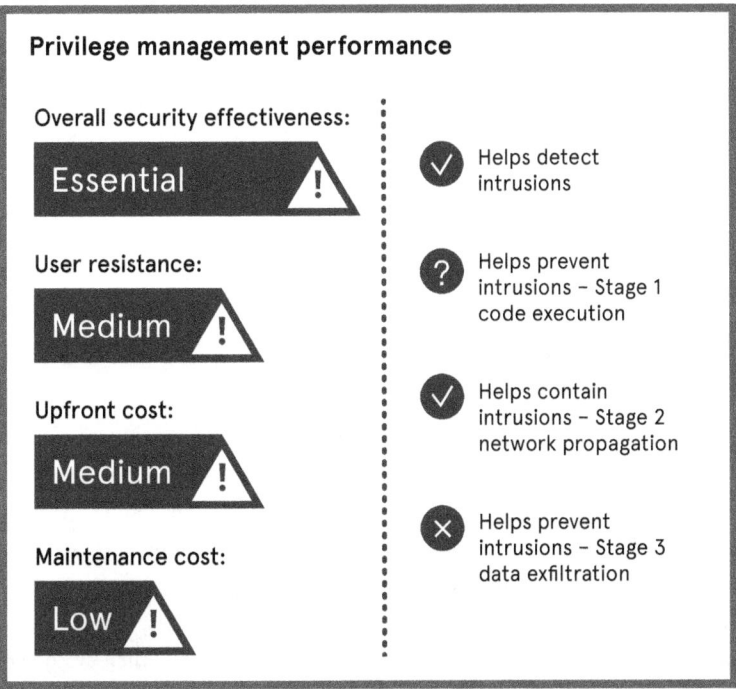

Finally, it is not enough to handle "in memory" attacks and you cannot entirely protect an operating system or user data. Of course, nothing is 100% and Application Whitelisting can be a huge step forward. Unfortunately, the difficulty in setting it up has meant it has not been widely adopted, especially on endpoints that require a lot of flexibility.

4.3. Standard Secure Configurations – typical tools and tech

Manufacturers and resellers often ship operating systems and devices with default configurations aimed at ease-of-deployment and ease-of-use, not security. Basic controls, open services and ports, default accounts or passwords, older (vulnerable) protocols, pre-installation of unneeded software - all of these can be exploitable in their default state.

To prevent attackers from exploiting vulnerable services and settings, establish, implement, and actively manage (track, report on, correct) the security configuration of laptops, servers, and workstations using a rigorous configuration management and change control process. Once again, bodies such as SANS, GCHQ, CESG, NIST and CPNI recognise this as a fundamental step in securing your environment.

HOW CAN GROUP POLICY HELP?

When it comes to configuring a large number of machines, Group Policy is a great and effective tool for ensuring a standard configuration across the estate. Group Policy is an infrastructure that allows you to implement specific configurations for users and computers. Settings are contained in Group Policy objects (GPOs), which are linked to the following Active Directory service containers: sites, domains, or organisational units (OUs). The settings within GPOs are then evaluated by the affected targets, using the hierarchical nature of Active Directory. Consequently, Group Policy is one of the top reasons for deploying Active Directory because it allows you to manage user and computer objects.

Many IT professionals incorrectly think Group Policy can be used to remove access to part of the system or settings. Essentially, all you are doing is "hiding" settings and options from the user. If the user has Administrative rights, they can simply access the setting by finding the applications and manually launching it or navigating to the registry and disabling Group Policy.

Another misconception amongst IT professionals is the belief that admin privileges can be assigned to applications via Group Policy. This is incorrect. You can manage group membership, giving people administrative rights etc, but you cannot assign privileges to applications with GPOs. I will explain later how permissions on files, folders and registry keys can be managed via GPOs, but this is distinctly different.

Group Policy is not foolproof

Group Policy is not completely watertight and when running as an administrator, Group Policy (and other secure controls) can be evaded in seconds. However, it's still possible to find your way around Group Policy even as a standard user. Windows applications are responsible for enforcing their own Group Policy settings. Standard users have full permissions over the processes they own, so there is the potential for one running process to modify another to ignore Group Policy. Therefore, you need to implement the following configuration recommendations to help secure it. However, as with most things, these settings result in a trade-off against us ability or affect system performance.

- Set the system boot order to ensure boot is from the local hard disk
- Set a BIOS password to prevent users from changing system files by booting into another OS
- Encrypt the system volume using BitLocker for the highest level of security
- Use SRP or AppLocker to block unknown applications from running
- Assign users read-only mandatory user profiles so they cannot override managed settings
- Group Policy processing can be configured to reapply settings, even if policy hasn't been changed since the last refresh

SUMMARY – IT'S GOOD, BUT ARDUOUS TO MAINTAIN

Developing configuration settings with good security properties is a complex task beyond the ability of individual users, requiring analysis of potentially hundreds or thousands of options in order to make good choices.

Even if a strong initial configuration is developed and installed, it must be continually managed to avoid security "decay" as software is updated or patched, new security vulnerabilities are reported, and configurations are "tweaked" to allow the installation of new software or the support of new operational requirements.

Attackers will find opportunities to exploit both network-accessible services and client software.

4.4. Patching – typical tools and tech

Unpatched applications are vulnerable to attack. By applying patches quickly and keeping them up to date, you close the door to malware and hackers looking to exploit flaws in your adopted software. Technology exists to proactively scan for vulnerabilities and address known flaws to reduce the risk of systems being compromised. Patches can be installed to a per-user directory, to allow a standard user application to directly patch files. Automated tools are used to create and maintain inventories of each device and applications used by an organisation. SANS, GCHQ, CESG, NIST, ADoD and CPNI see this as a key defence, because research has shown that 99.9%[3] of vulnerabilities were compromised a year after the CVE was published.

WINDOWS UPDATE SERVICES (WSUS)

Windows Server Update Services (WSUS) is a Microsoft tool that allows administrators to manage the distribution of updates and hotfixes released for Microsoft products to computers in a corporate environment. WSUS downloads these updates from the Microsoft Update website and then distributes them to computers on a network. WSUS runs on Windows Server and is free to licensed Microsoft customers. It includes many benefits, including download optimisation and central control of updates and patches.

---

3 Verizon DBIR 2015

SUMMARY – FIND A WAY TO STAY UP TO DATE!

Understanding and managing vulnerabilities requires significant time, attention, and resources. Some automated patching tools may not detect or install certain patches. If installed on a per-user basis, patches need to be re-downloaded per user, wasting time and hard drive space. What's more, on its own it is unable to track, trace and destroy attacks. There have been negative reports that patches cause systems not to boot. In addition, they are unable to prevent attacks to applications and the system at large.

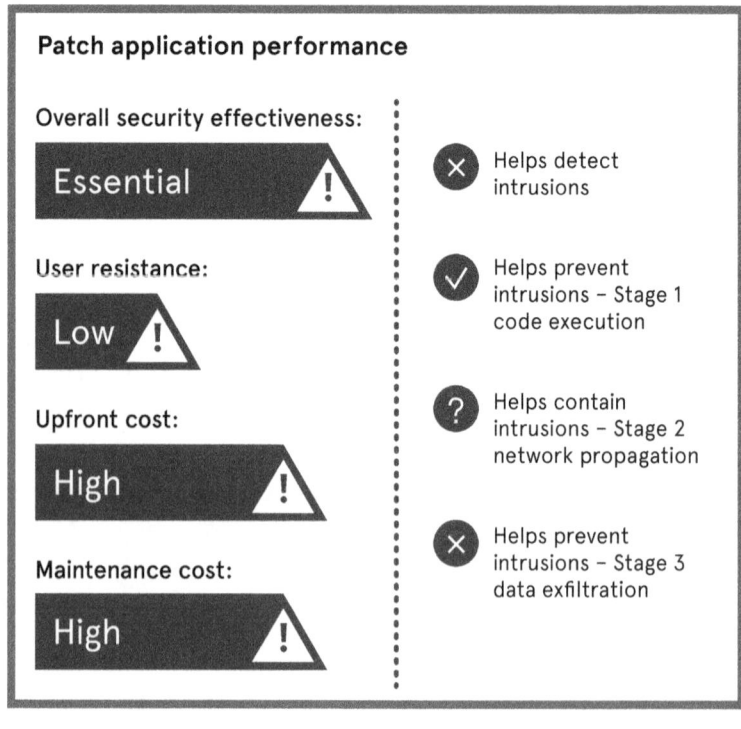

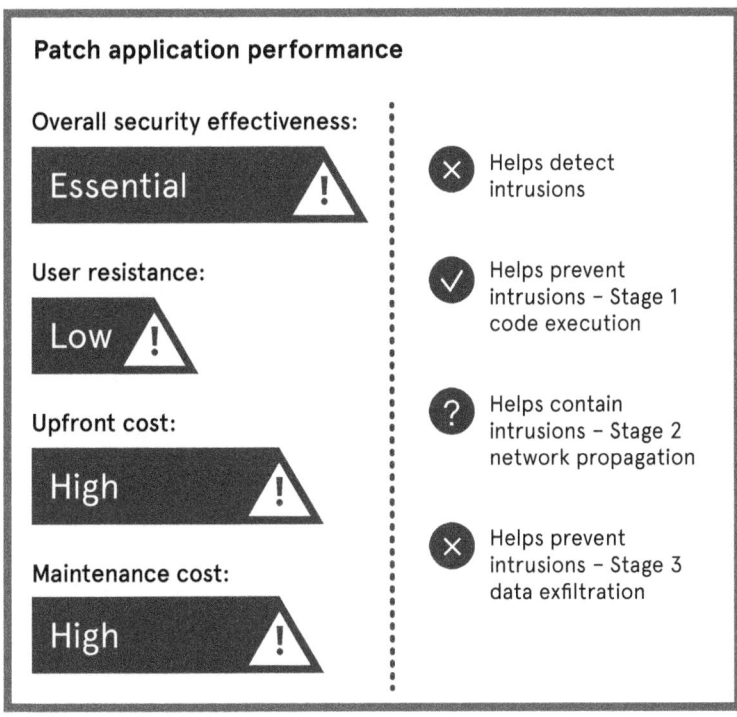

Another issue to take into account is the vast array of software used at organisations. Third party applications will not be managed by automation tools like WSUS, meaning you will need to track and manage updates manually. The problem is compounded when you do not have application control, as users introduce threats all the time, increasing the attack surface.

PART TWO

Technology to Achieve Defence in Depth

| 5 | Protection that works | 98 |
| 6 | Defence in Depth and your bottom line | 123 |

CHAPTER 5
Protection that works

5.1.	Privilege management	101
5.2.	Secure standard configuration	104
5.3.	Application control is easy (trust me!)	105
5.4.	Detection is dead – sort of	108
5.5.	Patch, patch! Oh – and patch!	112
5.6.	Sandboxing – let's not forget about Zero Day exploits	113
5.7.	Endpoint behavioural analysis	117
5.8.	Summary – perceptions of defence in depth	119

The key to any security posture should be a proactive "Defence in Depth" strategy. No security solution offers 100% protection, so you need to have a multi-layered approach to tackle modern threats and remain relevant in a constantly evolving landscape. This is DiD and to do it effectively, you need to prioritise key strategies - such as patching, privilege management and application whitelisting - and place them at the heart of your security design. Done right, DiD can actually yield results extremely fast. Layering multiple strategies makes initial penetration much harder for attackers, both externally and internally, and reduces the potential for privilege escalation if an account is compromised. The temptation exists for IT and security professionals to deploy the easiest and most familiar technologies first. Yet in the modern age of cyber threats, this is not the most effective use of resources and businesses should invest in those measures proven to provide the most control against the riskiest threat vectors.

The DiD strategy I am proposing here is not based on detection or blacklists. It delivers on the security foundations discussed in chapter 2 through proactive technologies. I will explain how security and freedom can be achieved by layering technologies that can actually be implemented. In chapter 7, I will delve into specifics on how these technologies can be configured.

THE ENDPOINT SECURITY PARADOX

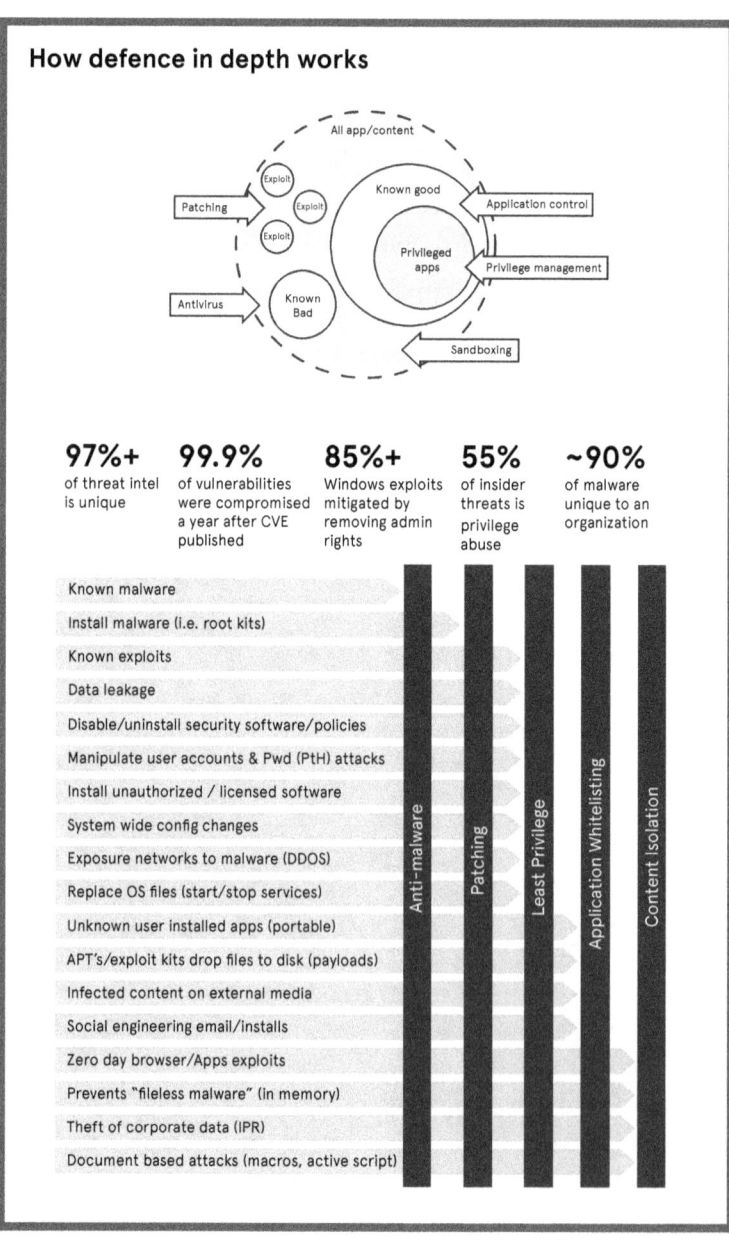

5.1. Setting foundations with privilege management

We know that reducing administrative rights is the single most effective thing you can do to reduce the Windows attack vector, mitigating the risk posed by 85% of critical vulnerabilities reported by Microsoft[1]. The use of standard accounts instead of administrative rights immediately increases your security protection, giving malware nowhere to go. Without the administrative rights it seeks, these threats cannot reach the core network, where they cause the most damage, or gain access to your corporate data.

You also need to implement privilege management technology that allows you to remove administrative rights and deal with the challenges of standard accounts. To be successful, it must have the capability to assign rights directly to applications, tasks, scripts and installers rather than to users (importantly this must work for both desktops and servers). This means you can allow all users to run with standard user accounts, protecting the operating system from internal and external threats that seek to exploit administrative rights. However, your users have the flexibility they need to be productive in their job roles, as discussed in Chapter 3.

In addition, by removing administrative rights you can maintain the integrity of your endpoint build/configuration (often referred to as the "Gold Standard" build) by first securing it. Standard users do not have the power to change it. Users will then require a granular and flexible policy overlaid, which allows specific and detailed changes to be made.

---

1   Microsoft Vulnerabilities Report 2015

WORKSHEET

The privilege management solution you choose must be able to:	
Replace UAC prompts with customisable messaging, ensuring that users are able to quickly and easily request the access as they need it.	
Provide insight and trend analysis reporting.	
Broad application type support.	
Flexible exception handling capabilities. Even with a good understanding of your users' needs there will be exceptions that crop up. Dealing with these through features like "break the glass" code and authorisation prompts will be key.	
Scale policies easily with firewall-style rules engines. This allows for clear and logical management and reduced management overheads.	
Integrate into existing infrastructure to allow quick and scalable deployments (such as Microsoft Group Policy or McAfee ePO).	

ATTACK VECTORS MITIGATED BY PRIVILEGE MANAGEMENT

As previously discussed, removing administrative rights is the single biggest thing you can do to secure a Windows endpoint. It mitigates 85% of the security vulnerabilities Microsoft released in 2015 and is backed up by a number of industry studies. I have complied a list of the attack vectors mitigated by the removal of administrative rights to help paint the picture of its importance.

- Install spyware and adware
- Install kernel-mode root kits
- Install system-level level key loggers
- Install ActiveX controls, including IE and Explorer extensions
- Install and start services
- Stop existing services (such as the firewall)
- Access data belonging to other users
- Replace OS and other program files with Trojan horses
- Disable/uninstall anti-virus virus
- Create and modify user accounts
- Reset local passwords
- Pass the Hash (PtH) attacks
- Render the machine unbootable
- Exposure of entire networks to malware, viruses, and denial-of-service (DOS) attacks
- Data corruption or manipulation
- System wide configuration changes
- Leakage of sensitive data
- System access and malware embedding in the OS

- Disabling security features/products
- Hiding files from user
- Installing drivers and services
- System wide persistence (HKLM run keys etc)
- Disabling administrator applied policy
- Access other users files
- Malware exploiting administrative rights
- UAC bypass attempts
- Malware installing outside of user profile
- Majority of insider threats are related to privilege abuse. Privilege Management prevents users from covering their tracks or abusing the system as much.

5.2. Focus on secure, standard configuration

There are many ways to ensure standard configuration on an endpoint, Group Policy being one. However, whatever method you choose, there is always a way to change settings if the user has administrative rights. A big advantage of standard user accounts is the fact that they aid change and configuration management. When an administrator logs onto a machine there is the potential that the system's configuration may undergo unsanctioned changes. A Privilege Management solution helps to maintain the intended configuration of a system, but at the same time gives the flexibility to change sanctioned items (if a Privilege Management solution allows).

Least privilege security enables system administrators to maintain better standardised environments and reduce support costs. If the service desk can be certain of a system's configuration, it is much easier to support that system. If users can make changes to important configuration settings, the help desk faces a much tougher job, increasing the time required to resolve problems, thus driving up costs.

Least privilege security also prevents users from circumventing controls implemented by system administrators. If a user has Administrative rights, with enough knowledge, it is possible to circumvent any security solution. Ultimately, if a user has administrative rights, there is likely a way to break into a system even if other controls are in force.

Good change and configuration management provides stability. Computers do not stop working without a reason; normally something or someone made a change.

5.3. Application control is easy (trust me!)

Removing privileges should not be viewed as a panacea for all security-related problems. It is still possible that malware could install itself by exploiting an unpatched security vulnerability, which might have otherwise required administrative rights to install. In addition, there are thousands of applications that are designed in a portable or a per-user form. These can be installed without administrative rights.

As a result, least privilege security cannot prevent all unauthorised software appearing on your network and should be used in conjunction with an Application Control solution. Malware could still infect a fully patched system running with least privilege. The damage would likely be limited to an individual user's profile, leaving the underlying system untouched. This damage limitation mechanism, provided by least privilege security, makes any malware outbreak on your network less serious and easier to clean up.

Privilege management then makes application whitelisting easy, by ensuring administrative rights can trust key areas of the build. This allows rules which trust the operating system, line of business applications and prohibits unauthorised applications.

Trusted Locations

- **Windows System (%systemroot%):** The operating system can be defined by the location and items signed within the Windows Security Catalog and therefore it is easy to identify and trust. Should OS functions trigger administrative rights they can be seamlessly elevated or the user prompted to enter an authorisation code by the Privilege Management solution.

- **Line of business applications (%programfiles%):** In most cases the trusted line of business applications will be installed in program files (other locations can also be defined) by either a deployment technology or a real administrator. In either case, the rules can be tweaked to allow an application in this location to run if it matches trusted criteria. For example, if an application has been digitally signed, installed by SCCM or a trusted administrator. Further rules can be applied to identify if it requires elevation and, if so, seamlessly elevate or prompt the user.

  > Look for a solution that can deal with complex parent and child scenarios. For example, should a trusted line of business application create and access files within the user temp directory, the solution must be able to establish if the parent process is trusted.

Untrusted locations

- User's profile (%userprofile%): There should be no reason why a line of business application would need to run for the user's profile. The profile is the only location the user has write access to once administrative rights have been removed. Therefore, malware and malicious users will try to exploit this location. Prohibiting the execution of code from here will thwart the vast majority of attacks

With this pragmatic approach to whitelisting, there is no need to create long lists of allowed applications, thus significantly reducing the deployment lifecycle.

If you analyse all the attacks over the last 12 months, most of them have tried to utilise administrative rights and drop a payload to disk. If the malware cannot utilise administrative rights or drop a payload to disk it is severely curtailed!

By implementing a flexible application whitelisting approach, good applications are allowed to execute and exceptions can be handled by providing multiple break the glass options, without compromising user experience or security. Look for a solution that combines Privilege Management and Application Control with the same rule set for ease of use.

ATTACK VECTOR MITIGATED BY APPLICATION CONTROL

I have included some worked examples of the types of attacks Application Control can prevent:

- Block executable payloads and scripts dropped to disk by exploited applications (Java, Flash, Adobe Reader etc.)
- Fake updates and files (Flashupdater2k.exe or springbreakpics.pdf.exe) from pop ups, email attachments and browsing
- APT's and exploit kits are almost always modular and drop files to disk
- Infected content on external media – USB, HDD, DVD etc containing malware executables
- Prevents payload stage of an attack (Stage 1 exploit vulnerability to gain RCE, Stage 2 drop and execute payload)
- Drive by downloads (malvertising, targeted attack, watering hole etc)
- Social engineering of the user ("run this for me", "install this" etc)
- Prevents unwanted applications being installed and introducing vulnerabilities (uTorrent etc)

5.4. Detection is dead – sort of

At a time when the IT environment is more diverse than ever, it is not enough to simply sit back and trust in reactive technologies, such as anti-malware, or detection based solutions. Anti-malware solutions simply cannot keep up with the volume of threats. 70-90% of malware is unique to your organisation – meaning it is highly targeted and therefore unknown to anti-malware vendors.[2] Anti-malware technologies are fighting a losing battle against an increasingly sophisticated malware

---

2   2015 Data Breach Investigations Report, Verizon, April 2015

threat landscape. Attackers often penetrate user endpoints with new malware that eludes the detection tools. One example is the release of BOOTRASH – a bootkit virus from FIN1 that executes before the OS boots. Fileless malware, which hides in the Microsoft Windows registry and deletes all traces of itself from the file system, has also grown in number.

While 92% of organisations have up-to-date anti-malware software in use today, only 34% rate it as effective in preventing cyber intrusions, according to Ponemon's 'Cyber Strategies for Endpoint Defence 2014' report. When I refer to anti-malware I'm referring generally to all detection technologies, such as antivirus, Host and network based IPS. In its '5 Reasons Why Your Antivirus Software is not Enough' report, Trend Micro claimed that the software often struggles against sophisticated threats, such as ZACCESS malware, which keeps malware routines out of plain sight.

What's more, anti-malware is traditionally built around reactive blacklisting, which APTs are able to bypass to move within a network without protection. IDG Connect explained that malware makers have found a way to circumnavigate blacklisting and create more bad software than good within a system. Known as morphing, once a virus is written, it changes so that one virus looks different to anti-malware software. In the modern cyber security environment, anti-malware also doesn't offer protection against internal threats. Admin users are able to disable and override anti-malware settings, leaving systems vulnerable to internal attacks and breaches.

The Eggshell theory – The latest incarnation of detection

As I mentioned at the start of the book, I have seen many organisations invest in perimeter technology to contain or block threats before they hit the endpoint. This technology, such as network-based detection and sandboxing, has a part to play but the problem is that if you do not secure the endpoints first, you end up with an eggshell security stance, where you are reliant on a single outer shell to protect your data. Without secure endpoints, even one small crack in your defences will leave you exposed.

When you look at some of the big US data breaches, a number had bought into the latest and greatest "next gen" network security technologies, which had "detected" the threats and raised warnings. The problem was that there was so much noise generated by the solutions that no one prevented the attacks happening, as thousands of other alerts flooded in daily. This is part of the battle when you are looking to detect threats, especially at a network level. It can be like looking for a needle in a haystack.

Network defences face an almost impossible trade-off between security and usability. You want threats to be deeply analysed, but you cannot make the user wait. This results in rash decisions being made by the solution, or network security features being disabled. Intel Security found that over 30% of organisations disable network-based security features in order to boost speed. Malware authors know this and therefore will create attacks that simply lay dormant for a period of time to bypass the network sandbox.

> **Malware has rapidly evolved to evade network Sandboxes using a variety of techniques including:**
>
> - Delayed onset
> - Detecting virtualised environment
> - Checking the number of CPU cores (network sandbox usually only presents one)
> - Checking if user is real (monitor mouse movement etc)
> - Exploiting the virtual environment to escape

If we do not believe the hype and accept that no system is ever 100% secure, we accept that some threats will not be detected – so where will these end up? On the endpoint.

If the endpoint is not robustly secured using proactive DiD, you are reliant on endpoint detection, such as AV, to block the threats - essentially the same kind of detection that failed to identify the threat at the network level. In this case, it only takes one threat to breach an organisation; one APT that is not detected and you are breached. In fact, when you look at a lot of network-based solutions they have accepted this fact and are now looking to detect attacks post compromise.

Possibly the most worrying aspect of network-based security is that some major network security vendors have been found to be introducing vulnerabilities and back doors into organisations. Several independent security researchers have detailed flaws that can be exploited by attackers to not only bypass these defences, but also gain access to a privileged position on the network.

Let us not forget that the corporate network is not the only way into a system. Mobile users who connect to external networks, USB devices or rogue users can all cause serious damage. How well does a network solution prevent these common attack vectors?

Critical business data is accessed and/or stored on the endpoint. This is where code - either good, bad or unknown – executes and has access to your data.

Network security products are often viewed as a panacea to the latest threats an organisation is battling with. Buy a box, plug it in and wait for a wonderful report that tells you how many threats are blocked. This might seem like a great solution, but in practice it just serves to give the illusion of a problem solved. Detection still has a part to play but it only becomes valuable and relevant once your IT staff have the capability to exert control over your enterprise network. Generally, its potency is reducing and if you rely too heavily on it, it may leave you exposed.

5.5. Patch, patch! Oh - and patch!

Patching is another very important part of DiD and it is still the best way to plug known code vulnerabilities. In its 'Labs Threat Report, November 2015', McAfee named patches as one of the best defences against macro malware attacks. By applying patches quickly and keeping them up to date, you close the door for malware and hackers to exploit flaws in your adopted software. Technology exists to proactively scan for vulnerabilities and address known flaws to reduce the risk of systems being compromised. Microsoft provides patch management automation within the OS.

According to research from CIO, 50% of chief information officers considered out of date security patches to be the number one threat to their security in 2015.[3] However, many organisations overlook the need to handle time dependant exceptions. Understanding and managing vulnerabilities requires significant time, attention, and resources. Some automated patching tools may not detect or install certain patches. On their own they are unable to track, trace and destroy attacks.

When administrative rights have been removed users will no longer be able to apply ad hoc, user initiated, patches. This highlights a need for a privilege management solution that can enable the elevation of update packages for applications without the need for administrative rights.

In addition, it is not always practical or quick for a large organisation to keep all of its endpoints fully patched, due to compatibility and geographical diversity. This poses the question of 'how do we protect trusted applications when patches do not exist or cannot be applied?'.

---

3   http://www.cio.com/article/2896715/security0/1-cyber-security-threat-to-information-systems-today.html

Patching helps reduce the noise and known threats which have long since been fixed.

5.6. Sandboxing - let's not forget about zero day exploits

Once the above technologies are in place, you need to turn your attention to zero day exploits in the known good (trusted) apps. This is where content isolation comes in. Content isolation - or sandboxing as it's often known - protects you from unknown threats and zero day attacks that might exploit a vulnerability before it's closed by a patch.

Application content runs in a secure sandbox, protecting the user, the endpoint, your data and the network. Sandboxing can be tricky to get off the ground as it often relies on heavyweight virtualisation or fails to address all entry points. Whatever solution you choose it's important that the sandbox builds on the technologies you have already invested in and deals with content originating from outside your organisation, not just the web.

Look for solutions that are lightweight and compatible with your existing security stack. In a similar way to how the Windows security model works, identify solutions that isolate each user's applications (processes) and data from one another, and standard users from the operating system core.

The solution should run applications running in the isolated sandbox as:

a) a different user

b) with minimum administrative rights

c) with standard user integrity

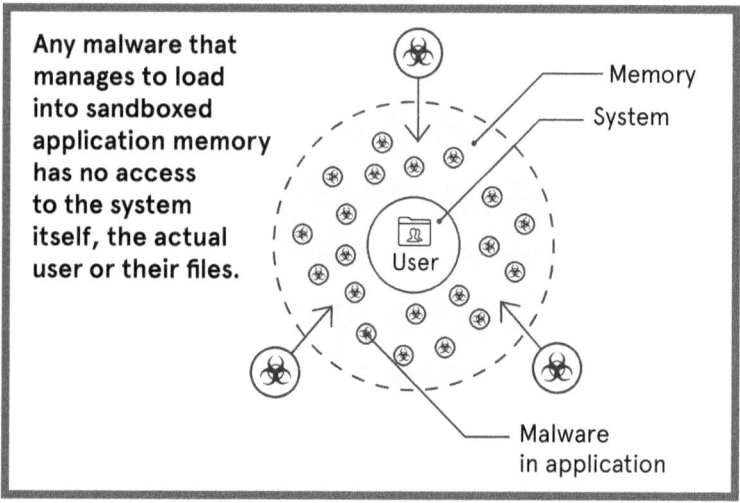

Any malware that manages to load into sandboxed application memory has no access to the system itself, the actual user or their files.

Attacks seeking system (kernel) access or access to user data outside the Sandbox will not succeed unless privilege escalation can be carried out in the memory of the sandboxed application process.

Malware running as the "sandbox" user is seriously restrained as it can't:

- Interact with the real user's processes or process memory - insufficient administrative rights
- Access the real user's files on the host or across network drives – insufficient administrative rights and authorisation
- Interact with 'the system' - Insufficient administrative rights and integrity
- Interact with system processes or memory
- Access the secure registry

- Access secure software installation locations (c:\windows\system32, c:\program files etc)
- Hijack user tokens of other users to start applications as another user – insufficient administrative rights running as standardd user
- Authenticate to any secured network endpoint (file shares, computers, etc) – running as a local account with no network administrative rights
- Launch unauthorised applications, whether it's on the host already (eg cmd.exe) or newly downloaded – heightened application execution control applied to Sandboxed apps

ATTACK VECTORS MITIGATED BY SANDBOXING

Sandboxing provides a great way of controlling what a piece of malware can do, including:

- Java Exploits
- Flash Exploits
- Browser zero day
- PDF based attacks, active script and assorted vulnerabilities leading to RCE
- Document based attacks, macros, script and threats such as Sandworm
- Provide a unique context for strict app control. No cmd, no PowerShell etc prevents "fileless malware",, such as Powerliks running scripts from in memory or registry
- Reduces remediation costs for restoring after an attack
- IP theft or ransomware blocked from accessing private data

Context aware application control

An important point to make here is that, with the right products, sandboxing can be very easily combined with tight application control. If we look at Internet Explorer running within the sandbox, for instance, there should be no need for it to execute command and control executables or run applications which are not part of its normal behaviour. Therefore, it is very easy to create tight controls for applications running inside the sandbox.

An example of this is the Poweliks Trojan horse that installs as a fileless threat and performs click-fraud operations. The threat installs itself into the Windows registry where it changes existing CLSID entries to run itself when certain Windows functions are performed.

Once installed, Poweliks will contact command and control (C&C) servers to download further instructions. In some cases additional infections may be released, due to the downloading of malicious adverts (malvertisement) leading to exploit kits.

 Look for a solution that can bring together all of these concepts into a single pane of glass.

5.7. Endpoint behavioural analysis

In addition to the above controls, your organisation will require detailed auditing and reporting which can provide trend analysis (including detailed application access, application elevation, application execution prevention and sandboxing) and a mechanism to simplify rule creation.

Good reporting should incorporate a rich set of preconfigured dashboards and reports, including executed applications, elevated applications, blocked applications and discovered applications. The dashboards should provide detailed summaries of unique applications and processes, including the user and computer where they were executed. Trend analysis reports help to highlight patterns, behaviours and peak usage. The timeframe for the data displayed on a dashboard can be switched between 24 hours, 7 days, 30 days and 12 months, with advanced filtering options enabling granular customisation of reports. Application and process summaries provide an additional broad overview of their usage across the enterprise. Applications can also be grouped by application type, publisher, policy, application group, users and groups or by host.

The below areas are of specific importance:

User experience

Understanding user experience will enable you to identify how your users have been interacting with the solution by itemising those which received blocking and elevation messages. If a user is seeing too many prompts this will present a poor user experience. Having good visibility will help you tweak your policies to avoid this.

Application monitoring

Look for a solution that provides insight into:

- **Privileged applications:** Reports on all applications that have been executed with elevated rights, including a breakdown of applications that were elevated automatically and those that were elevated via exception handling.

- **Blocked applications:** Reports on all applications that were blocked as a result of Whitelisting and/or Blacklisting policies.

- **Passive monitoring:** Reports all application usage across protected endpoints to aid software licensing and applicable compliance mandates

Discovery

Insight into all applications that require administrative rights versus those that don't will help with policy design. Trend analysis should be included, which provides items like the Top 10, most used applications and most discovered publishers. Look for a solution that has good integration between reporting and the policy engine to aid policy design.

Deployment statistics

To aid deployment, the solution should provide detail around clients that are currently deployed, including the total number of endpoints. Detailed summaries of OS family, device type and language, all help with tracking agent rollouts and updates.

Policy coverage

To support policy management, the solution must provide policy usage across all managed endpoints, highlighting where policies are taking effect, as well as summarising policies by activity. Coverage reports should show the most and least active policies in terms of user and host coverage, as well as application and process enforcements. Policy summaries should provide detailed statistics on individual activity relating to users and hosts managed by a policy, and related trend analysis.

Tamper protection

The solution should provide reporting on any users who have attempted to circumvent the system, by trying to manipulate groups and users. This report must breakdown attempts by user, computer, the application used and also the individual privileged groups that were protected.

5.8. Summary - perceptions of defence in depth

The endpoint should be where you start when looking to secure your enterprise against the latest APTs and cyber threats. From here, you can build out. To understand why we do this, remember that a bank does not leave the vault door open just because it has a security guard on the door. In a business, data and IP is money – so as reassuring as it is to have something watching data coming in and out, if you don't secure the endpoint you risk losing it all.

I have discussed the above approaches with lots of IT professionals who initially expressed concern about the capabilities of a DiD approach. Many worried about layering heterogeneous technologies in an environment, as it often leads to extensive administrative overhead. The perceived labour-intensive nature of DiD has also resulted in concerns about productivity, as its success or failure often depends on those managing and maintaining it. Owners, boards of directors and C-level executives pile on the pressure for IT professionals to protect systems Four out of five IT professionals were made to roll out projects despite them not being ready due to security issues. The need to introduce tech with all of the latest features was also prominent, even if there were not the resources in place to deal with it. What's more, there seems to be a lack of awareness when it comes to security strategies. For any strategy to be successful there needs to be cooperation, commitment and skill across anorganisation. Staff at all levels need to understand security policies and the part they play in security measures to prevent individuals falling prey to schemes such as phishing emails.

According to the Department for Business, Innovation and Skills, in the UK 42% of large organisations do not offer any ongoing security awareness training to staff. 93% of companies claim that where the security policy was poorly understood, staff-related breaches occurred.[4]

Part of the problem is that there is not currently enough emphasis placed on the user. Ponemon's 'Cyber Strategies for Endpoint Defense' report found that end users were not high on cyber security agendas. Only 9% of respondents claim user experience is important when rolling out an information security project, which can create challenges in terms of user adoption and satisfaction.[5]

---

4   https://data.gov.uk/data/resource_cache/8e/8ea4e75e-19f9-49f7-bc9d-5a5b688d12aa/bis-13-p184-2013-information-security-breaches-survey-technical-report.pdf
5   http://www.ponemon.org/local/upload/file/Cyber%20Strategies%20for%20Endpoint%20Defense%20Final1.pdf

By now hopefully you can see the benefits of layering the technologies I described in this section. However, you may not be convinced it is possible to combine all the technologies without a lot of work and without it affecting the end user. I would share your concerns if it were not for two reasons; 1) I've done it hundreds of times and 2) the core of your fear will centre around the perceived difficulty of implementing privilege management, application whitelisting and sandboxing, which is no longer the challenge it once was. Like anti-virus and patching, which are well understood and can be simply automated, solutions now exist that allow privilege management, application whitelisting and sandboxing to be managed centrally via a single agent.

Furthermore, the management of these next generation tools can be integrated into existing management platforms such as Active Directory. This is the key to making this approach simple and easy.

Let's put the importance of DiD into context. If a piece of malware is not allowed to execute due to unknown applications being blocked there is not much it can do. If it is allowed to execute, due to an exploit in a trusted application, it will have no administrative rights to exploit and no access to your data as it is isolated. When it comes to a cyber attack, the earlier in the cyber kill chain you can prevent an attack, the more effective the defence. A proactive approach allows you to realise this benefit by not waiting until malware is running or spreading across the network to stop it. Instead, you isolate any potentially vulnerable line of business applications to mitigate threats.

All of this can now be achieved whilst still allowing users to experience a rich and free operating environment. In part three I discuss the implementation methodology that brings all this together.

Real world: Security will fail or be circumvented if the user experience is not at the centre of its design. If security gets in the way and users can not do their job, security will be weakened or turned off completely. I have seen this time and time again at enterprises large and small. Do not underestimate the power of the end user.

CHAPTER 6

Defence in Depth and your bottom line

6.1. Security recommendations from external experts   124

6.2. Don't believe me? Try it for yourself!   127

A key challenge when it comes to determining ROI for security solutions is that many of the benefits are hard to quantify in purely financial terms. This is because much of the damage caused by cyber attacks cannot be easily be communicated via a balance sheet - at least in the short-term.

While immediate costs such as monetary fines, compensation, lost business during downtime and fees charged by external experts to rectify problems are measureable, the hit to a business' reputation, Intellectual Property and competitive advantage is much more intangible, and potentially more significant.

 In 2015, 41% of IT and business executives rated the damage to their reputation as the single biggest impact of a cyber security incident - up from 30% the previous year.[1]

---

1   2015 Information Security Breaches Survey, BIS/PwC, June 2015

Striking the balance between security and freedom brings with it a multitude of benefits, not least of which is a dramatic reduction is TCO (Total Cost of Ownership). This is achieved through the reduced demand on the helpdesk and reduced user down time.

While my experience shows that implementing a DiD security strategy on the endpoint brings with it security, user enablement and financial benefits, I do not want you to take my word for it. Fortunately, there is independent evidence from Gartner, Forrester and others that back up my experiences.

This book is not intended to justify a business case or ROI for proactive defence, but I will share a checklist of considerations that will help you to demonstrate savings in cost and productivity.

6.1. Security recommendations from external experts

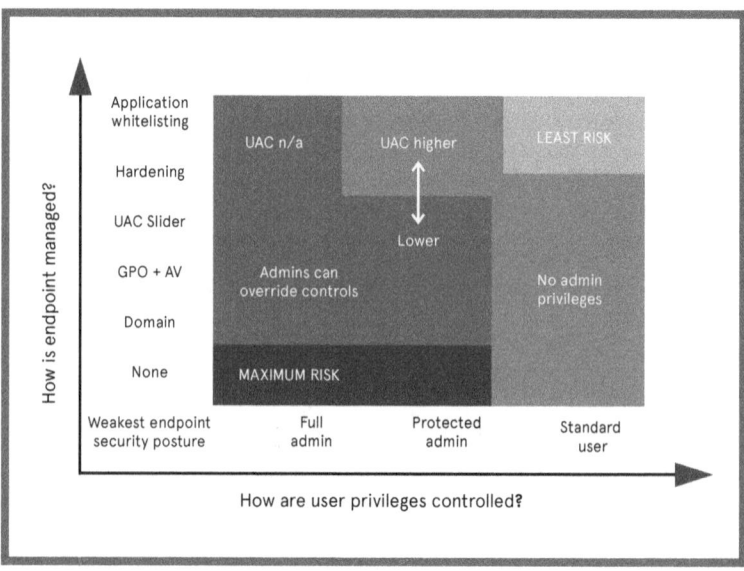

As you can see in this diagram, even implementing all the technologies up the vertical axis still leaves you exposed whilst performing the single step of removing administrative rights takes you out of the red. The goal is to get to the top right hand corner, but you won't be able to get there without an endpoint security technology.

When users are prevented from making unintentional changes to critical system components on the endpoint, the risk of malicious or unsanctioned software executing is significantly reduced. The likelihood of users being infected with drive-by internet attacks, rootkits, or worms is minimised as users need to specifically give permission for such software to run. A large number of malicious programs require administrative rights to cause any damage, so when removed, a standard user is far less likely to infect a machine accidentally. What's more, even if a standard user account becomes infected with a virus, the damage it can do is considerably less than if they had been granted administrative rights.

Another organisation that advocates a more holistic and proactive approach to security is Forrester. Endpoint analyst Chris Sherman, publishing a paper in 2014 entitled "Five alternatives to endpoint antivirus", explained that relying on detection alone leaves you with a large attack surface, whereas layering technologies moves you to a smaller attack surface.

 At the time of writing Netflix had removed AV entirely and is relying on other technologies to deal with APTs[2]

---

2   http://www.forbes.com/sites/thomasbrewster/2015/08/26/netflix-and-death-of-anti-virus/#38f5e19d3256

In Critical Security Controls for Effective Cyber Defense, the Council on Cyber Security listed whitelisting, blacklisting, secure configurations for hardware and software across multiple endpoints, continuous vulnerability assessment and remediation, and malware defences in its top five strategies. You can see the list below, but the multi-faceted nature of these recommendations stress the importance of adopting a DiD strategy.[3]

---

3   http://www.sans.org/reading-room/whitepapers/analyst/layered-security-works-34805

WORKSHEET

6.2. Don't believe me? Try it for yourself!

Combining my experiences with anecdotal evidence supporting the benefits of a DiD security strategy is all well and good, but I can imagine you are thinking: "My organisation is different, with unique requirements". The best way to persuade you and your management to test the theory is by carrying out a Proof of Concept. Running your own trials and comparing the following variables (before and after):

Number of application installation requests	
Software packages installed (manually by IT)	
Software packaging requests	
Active X installations	
Browser plugin installations	
Configuration of printers	
Desktop configuration & maintenance (Disk defrag etc.)	
Device connectivity (3G dongles etc.)	
Patch management	
Configuration of e-mail profiles	

Desktop power settings	
Desktop systems re-imaged (due to user error)	
New desktop deployments	
Writing or maintaining custom configuration scripts	
OS changes	
Managing admin group membership	
Blocking portable apps	

Running these tests will also give you some insight into the technical pre-requisites your organisation has and help you build a picture of the following proof points:

User satisfaction & productivity comparisons	
Number of helpdesk cases logged per month	
Number of helpdesk calls that are desktop/laptop related per month	
Number of helpdesk calls for administrative rights requests per month	
Number of helpdesk calls for UAC prompt confusion per month	
Number of unrequired Microsoft CALs	

Number of unrequired CALs from other providers	
Average resolution time for 1st line calls	
Average resolution time for 2nd line calls	
Average resolution time for 3rd line calls	
Average annual salary for 1st line helpdesk administrators	
Average annual salary for 2nd line helpdesk administrators	
Average annual salary for 3rd line helpdesk administrators	
Average annual salary for IT Security administrators	
Average annual salary for IT Desktop Management administrators	
Average annual travel expenditures for 3rd line support visits	

130

PART THREE

Implementation Success

7	Defence in Depth is great in theory – but how do I implement it?	132
8	Building group consensus	188
9	Tools and vendor selection	193
10	Final thoughts	210

CHAPTER 7
Defence in Depth is great in theory – but how do I implement it?

7.1.	The Implementation methodology	133
7.2.	Stage 1 – Design workshop (start with the end in mind)	135
7.3.	Stage 2 – Technology deployment	148
7.4.	Stage 3 – Requirements discovery (understanding your use case)	151
7.5.	Stage 4 – Data analysis & use case definition	157
7.6.	Stage 5 – Layering policies	165
7.7.	Stage 6 – Policy testing	172
7.8.	Stage 7 – Internal communication	176
7.9.	Stage 8 – Production deployment	180
7.10.	Stage 9 – Business as usual support (post deployment)	185

By now, you can hopefully see that prevention is possible. However, if you are like me your next logical thought will be "how do I implement this?"

During this chapter I will be bringing to life how DiD is possible. I have developed this six phase, nine stage implementation methodology based on my work with hundreds of customers. The project management principles come from PRINCE 2 and this methodology has proven to be secure and robust in the most demanding of environments. As a result I've been able to deploy DiD in some of the most diverse and largest organisations. For example, I deployed half a million endpoints with DiD in six months.

 The methodology is not set in stone and would normally be customised to meet the needs of the organisation - bear this in mind whilst reading.

7.1. The implementation methodology

The ownership of nine stages is split across the vendor and the customer and you can see from the diagram that two of the key stages - four and five - are very much within the vendor's court and these are crucial for project success (the size of the square denotes the effort involved). After each phase I make sure that it is signed off by the customer, thus ensuring you are completely satisfied with the work. You can also see from the bottom section of the diagram the teams that will be required for each of the phases in the deployment.

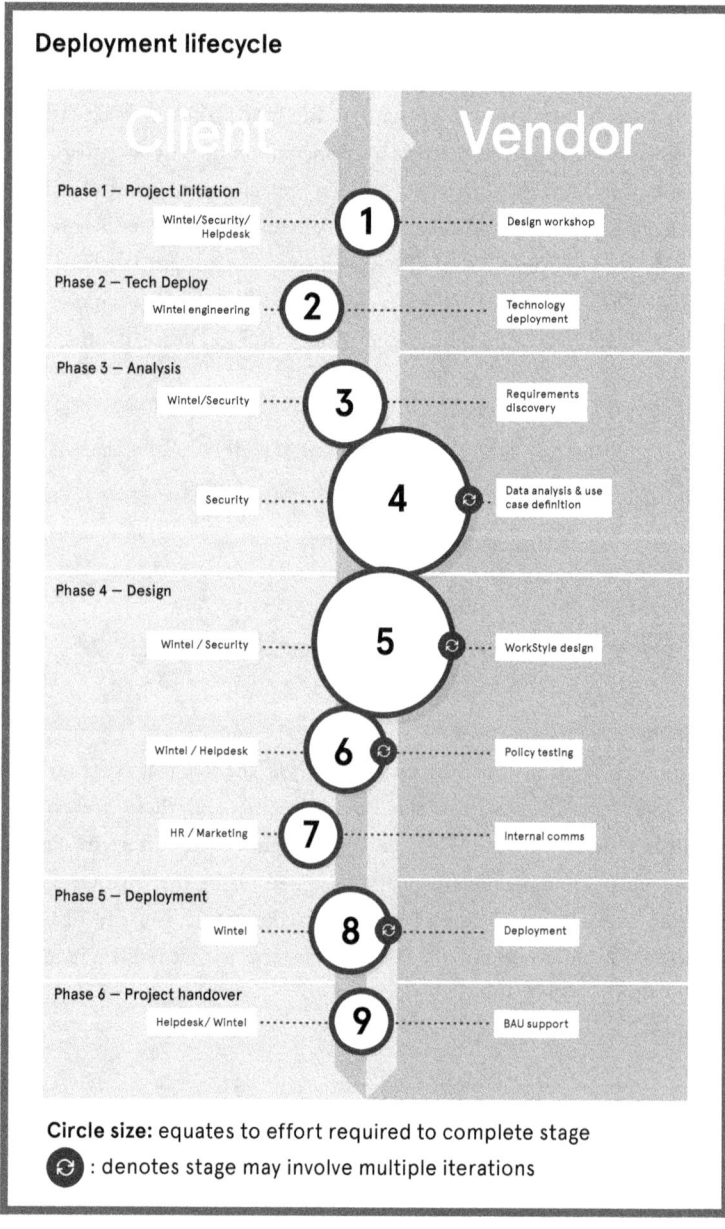

7.2. Stage 1 – Design workshop (start with the end in mind)

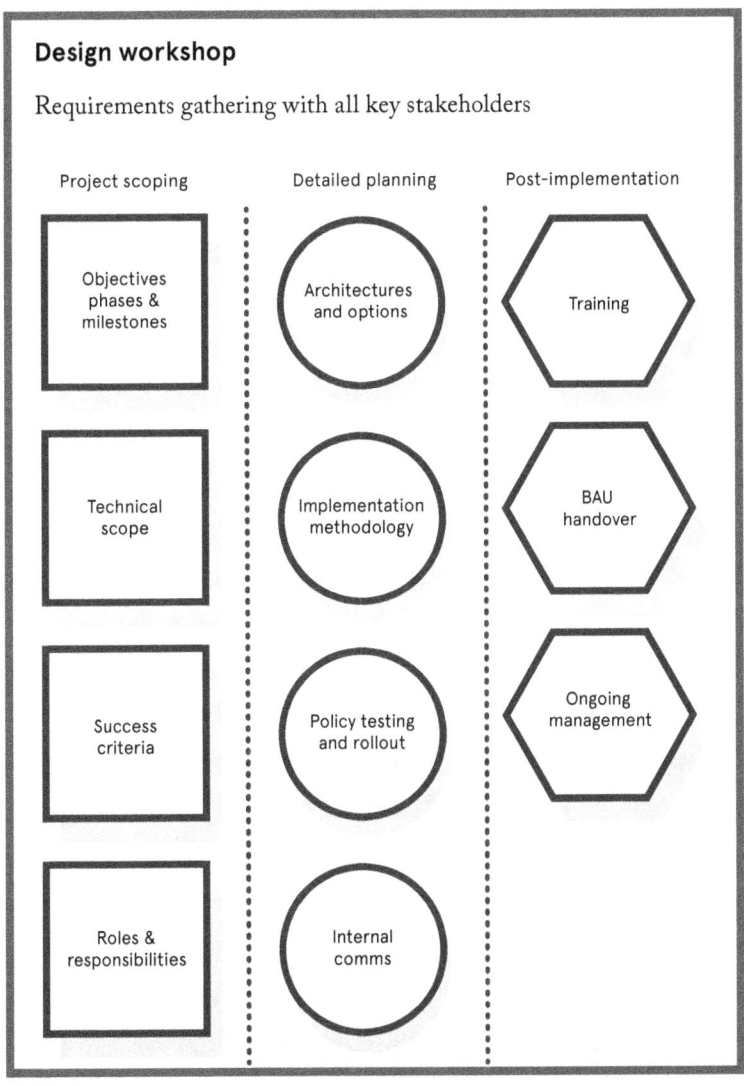

I place a significant emphasis on the design and planning stages of an implementation. In order for a detailed Project Initiation Document (PID) to be created, I would hold requirement gathering and design workshops with my clients to launch the project. This should ensure that the key stakeholders from across the business are involved from the outset, which is crucial for a successful adoption. During this consultation period, I will work closely with the stakeholders to agree the key points highlighted in the image above.

 I have seen projects fail where the technology has been imposed on the business.

Defining objectives – understanding why

It is important to start with the end in mind! Start with why you are running the project. Once the objectives have been discussed and requirements have been established, you can use these as key measurement criteria (milestones by which your project is measured). I have included a number of questions you can use to establish your requirements and help ascertain the insight you will need.

Business objectives:

- What is your approach to managing this risk based on your need to drive the business' profitability/and deliver against the board's objectives/agenda? How free can you afford your users to be?
- Do you have to meet any compliance mandates? external, internal quality/compliance/risk systems
- Is security seen as an enabler within your business or a box ticking exercise? Does your business believe you have achieved a ROI out of security in the last three years or is it just seen as mitigating risk?
- What is the board's view on cyber security risks?

- Do you benchmark your own security against your competitors?
- How do you strike a balance between security of assets and the need for employees to be productive?
- Have there been outbreaks which have resulted in data or productivity loss?

Environment questions

- What directory services are in use for endpoint management? E.g. Active Directory, McAfee ePO? Are all endpoints under the management scope of this technology?
- Do you have a delegate security model?
- Are IT operations centralised or decentralised?
- What Help desk / Service desk technologies do you use? E.g. Service Now?
- What is your current approach to User Account Control? Is this on, off or toned down?
- What software deployment technologies are currently in use, for example SCCM?
- Do you maintain a software inventory list and understand the privileges they require?
- How many diverse groups exist within your environment? E.g. developers, engineers?
- Are a number of these remote workers or do they spend a lot of time on the road?
- What is your approach to end user experience? Do you have a culture of a free and open environment or is it locked down and controlled?
- Which Windows operating system(s) is in place?
- Are you planning a migration to the latest versions of Windows? Desktop and servers?

- Which legacy Windows operating systems will you need to support? Desktop and servers?
- Do users have local administrative rights on the endpoint periodically, depending on the tasks at hand, or all the time?
- Do you have applications that require them to be a local administrator in order to run?
- Do you have users that need to install peripherals?
- Do you have users that need to install applications that require the user to be a local administrator?
- Do you have users that need to run built-in Windows features or functions that require the user to be a local administrator?
- Do you have a list of applications that you want to deny the user from running?
- Do you want to create an approved list of applications that users can run?

 I spent five days with a large global bank understanding their existing process and procedures and working out its policy landscape. Typically, this would be one to two days.

WHO SHOULD BE INVOLVED?

The project must be well thought out and planned accordingly as it will touch every endpoint in the environment. DiD solutions require more than just the desktop or server support team be involved, as this is typically not the only team that needs to support the solution and define the goals. Initially it is important to define the business sponsor(s) and project owner(s). These stakeholders are responsible for ensuring the project receives the funding and attention that it deserves, as well as driving and keeping the project on track.

At the start of the project, all stakeholders will need to be involved. I have provided a list below of the typical teams that would need to participate.

Stakeholder	Why Required
Security	The discussions will focus on a defence in depth security strategy. It is therefore important that the requirements of the security team are captured. This will enable the team to design a solution that meets the security standards within your organisation.
Infrastructure	Multiple deployment and management platforms will be discussed. Ongoing maintenance will also need to be performed by the appropriate team and this needs to be considered. The infrastructure teams will need to be consulted to ensure the most appropriate fit for your business.
Service Delivery	Whilst the technologies discussed, during the workshop, offer unparalleled security, they also deliver operational savings through end-user empowerment. Therefore it is important to understand the end-user issues related to overlocked or under locked environments. This data can be used to demonstrate operational savings.
Human Resources	On occasion, customers will engage with human resources before deploying security tools. There may be considerations around monitoring of users' activity or restricting what the user can or can't do with their computers. If such issues exist within your organisation we suggest attendance at the workshop by the appropriate representatives.

Client Platform	One of the most critical elements of any solution is how it is perceived by the end users. We suggest that representation from the client platform team is required to discuss what and how end-user communications will be delivered and how the technologies will be integrated into the endpoint platform.
Project Team	The project manager should be involved to ensure the smooth running of the process and that any subsequent actions are carried out. It is also normal practice for the project managers to co-ordinate with participants and ensure the appropriate facilities are available (meeting rooms, conference facilities etc.).

PROJECT MANAGEMENT

Defining ownership of the project and lines of communication, both internally and with the vendor, is crucial for success. It is vital that all members of the project team communicate efficiently and work effectively throughout every stage of the project. At a minimum, the following components should be in place during the project and implementation:

- Periodic project update meetings with all team members
- Weekly review of the issues log (this might need to include the vendor support)
- Identify training requirements and ensure training is conducted as soon as possible

DO I NEED A DESKTOP REFRESH TO DEPLOY DiD?

In short, the answer is no. Having said that, there are also sound technical justifications why you should consider installing a new OS image at the same time as implementing DiD. A fresh standardised image with built-in DiD allows us to ensure an issue-free experience, and provides additional benefits, such as the extra performance gained from a new install and elimination of undetected software and configuration errors.

If DiD is applied to an existing system you potentially freeze any existing configuration errors into the system and you may not see the full benefits.

THE CULTURE SHOCK

Understanding the nuances of company culture is crucial to the success of this type of project - or for that matter any project. I have seen company culture inhibit both innovation and change. People's natural response is to resist change, and this is no less true in the area of computer security, as users almost universally perceive security as an inconvenience which gets in the way of their user experience. However, it does not have to be this way. Security should be an enabler and hopefully you have seen through this book that the balance between security and freedom truly can be achieved.

UNDERSTANDING CULTURE

I have implemented DiD security strategies in a whole host of organisations, from those with a few employees to global enterprises with half a million employees. As you can imagine the gulf between these cultures is exponential. Obviously, this can affect what can be achieved, and how to go about doing it. Before embarking on a project of this sort you need to understand the culture as this will drive how the project will be conducted.

Company culture determines how the employees and management of a company behave. For instance, to what extent do employees:

- Help one another and contribute to teamwork?
- Co-operate to achieve common goals?
- Respect each other?
- Understand the work of colleagues in other departments?

If the answers to the above are positive then it's likely that your company has a healthy culture. This will make the project easier to implement, as employees will strive to understand why the project is being run.

If the answer is negative, employees may be defensive, unreasonable, have unrealistic expectations, or be aggressive. IT is likely to struggle to get users on side with any new project. However, all is not lost, for with the right solution, implementation plan and communication approach it is possible to make the project a success. However, it will take a little longer and need more care.

BUILD THE PLAN

Once the objectives, requirements, success criteria and team have been established the project plan can be created. This timeline will include the pilot, and all stages of the implementation methodology. The project timeline should also include time for project team training, internal communication and end user training. Additionally, there will need to be time allocated for post-implementation troubleshooting, Business As Usual handover and project closure.

PROJECT TIMELINE

Following the design workshop, I recommend creating a detailed project scope and Project Initiation Document (PID), clearly highlighting the finer details of the project so that all parties are clear on objectives and requirements. We can then establish milestones that will be used to sign off the project.

This will all form the basis of the project timeline. I typically recommend the initial stages of the project timeline should not overlap but once the team becomes more familiar with the implementation methodology phases, this can change. What's more, as the team becomes more experienced, the project will become easier.

Depending on the size and complexity of your organisation, as well as the complexity of the approval processes, a typical project can be as short as one month or as long as 12 months. I typically see projects averaging between three and six months.

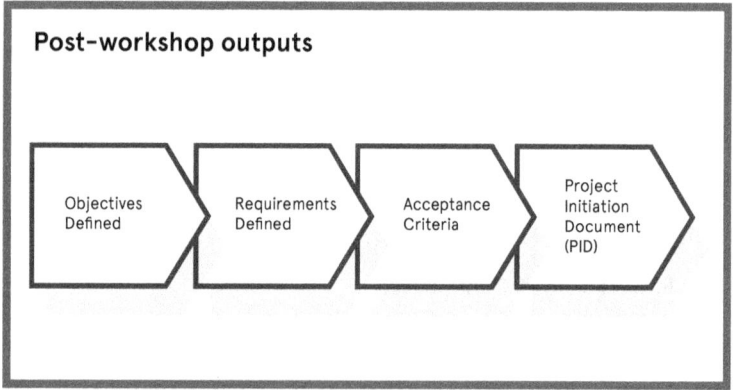

WHAT DOES SUCCESS LOOK LIKE?

There are a number of different vectors to define and measure success. During these coming sections I will discuss various factors that need to be taken into account.

BUY-IN FROM SENIOR MANAGEMENT

Ultimately success will be defined by user acceptance and support from management. A smooth and trouble-free implementation is in the interests of the business, and in the event that you should encounter resistance on the shop floor, it is good to know you have got full backing from management. No one likes being undermined and I often see projects fail when users push back and managers simply overrule IT.

Current financial and threat landscapes often play a part; if times are hard then the lowered TCO will help management get behind the project. If you have just been breached, then the security advantages need to be focused on.

IT'S LIKE SELLING INSURANCE AGAINST SHARK ATTACKS!

Security projects are often hard to sell and this is especially true when the business has little understanding of security beyond antivirus software and firewalls. Most corporate boards have no one sitting on them who comes from an IT background, being mainly made up of sales and finance experience. Consequently, they often assume that anti-malware and firewalls are enough.

Security is like selling insurance against shark attacks: No one understands why they need it until it is too late! The problem is, IT security is hard to quantify unless you have a background in computer science. After all, if management cannot see a problem (a shark), they are not worried about insuring against it. Security needs to be presented as a real business problem that affects the company's bottom line. Physical security is easy to see; everyone wants a lock on their front door as it is clear what the consequences are. What is the risk of not taking proactive action?

Cleaning up the damage after the attack is much harder and more costly than taking steps to reduce the risk of it happening in the first place.

MAP DiD TO BUSINESS KEY PERFORMANCE INDICATORS

Mapping security risks to KPIs helps to get acceptance from management for your DiD project. Showing management how DiD will help you better manage security incidents will allow the benefits of the project resonate. Avoid showing detailed statistics depicting the number of viruses prevented over a given time period but rather focus on how efficiently security is managed to ensure you don't detract from the holistic picture.

Nonetheless, looking at a list of KPIs and trying to map them to security issues could be a daunting task. Security incidents affect productivity, compliance and business continuity on a micro level, making it hard to map security risks to high-level KPIs. IT systems are so critical to the operation of most businesses that any risk introduced into the computer systems has the potential to affect a large number of a company's KPIs. For example, demonstrating how a security incident and its subsequent downtime will affect the team's ability to hit target. This shows that security is a business problem, and not just an IT issue.

I appreciate this is not easy and it is often the case that business KPIs simply do not map across. Consequently, I would recommend you create a set of KPIs based on how IT supports the business and it's processes. You will need to have a good knowledge of your business to fully understand the motivations for particular KPIs. However, this will not only affect your DiD project but how IT approaches supporting the business.

REDUCING COSTS

Demonstrate to management how future costs will be reduced by implementing a DiD project. The analyst data presented earlier will be helpful and data collected during Proof of Concepts and Pilots will help you relate this back to your environment.

SECURITY ADDS VALUE

Demonstrate to management that strong security helps business continuity and thus adds value. In the event of a serious virus outbreak, a DiD approach can help minimise or even prevent systems from crashing and being subject to data loss.

It is useful to include governance on how security decisions are made. Record by whom and how these are decided so, when security issues arise, it is clear who was ultimately responsible. If the decision to ignore key risk indicators was taken, it will be clear who made this decision.

AIM FOR 100%

Aim for 100% of your endpoint (desktops and server) to come under the scope of your DiD project! With the right tools and approaches in place (like those outlined in this book), there should be no reason why this is not achievable, in theory. The reality is, the real world is different; there will always be systems and users who are missed, for a myriad of reasons. The point here is aim high; I have extensive conversations with clients to establish at what percentage they will class the project as complete. With the right tools, you will be able to report on the number of users now running with standard rights vs administrative rights and so on.

7.3. Stage 2 – Technology deployment

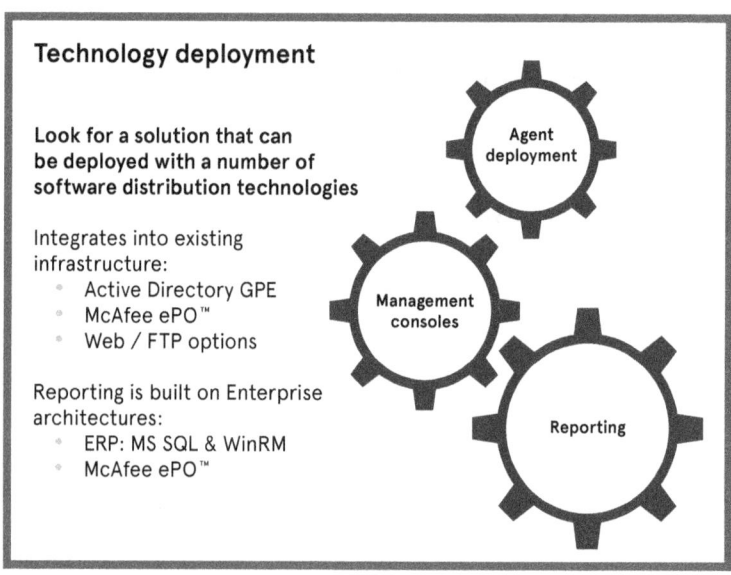

Technology deployment

Look for a solution that can be deployed with a number of software distribution technologies

Integrates into existing infrastructure:
- Active Directory GPE
- McAfee ePO™
- Web / FTP options

Reporting is built on Enterprise architectures:
- ERP: MS SQL & WinRM
- McAfee ePO™

At this point in the project you will have established your requirements; the next key stage is to make important architecture design decisions. While many solutions look to build their own proprietary systems to deploy policies and agents to the endpoints, this adds a significant management cost and a high learning curve. It is important to implement a solution that has tight integration with your existing infrastructure and provides multiple deployment options; such as Active Directory and Group Policy, McAfee ePO and Webservers. This gives many additional benefits, including hierarchical policy management and a strong security model that includes delegated administration.

There are three key areas to consider:

1. **Management console:** e.g. Group Policy, McAfee ePO / standalone version
2. **Agent deployment:** e.g. MSI package or McAfee ePO
3. **Reporting:** e.g. SQL databases, proprietary database

When working in large enterprises I often find that not all of the endpoints fall under the management scope of a single deployment architecture. Therefore, it is important to understand this earlier on in the design stages and plan accordingly. I would also recommend choosing a solution that ensures feature parity across deployment topologies. It is often the case trade-offs need to be made when deciding on architecture.

SEPARATION OF DUTY

In large enterprises it is most often the case that the security and operations responsibility is split across multiple teams. Therefore, it is important that your policy can be designed and transferred securely to the teams responsible for deployment. This is achieved by integrating into existing infrastructure, thus utilising the built in delegation models. In addition, look for solutions that have the ability to digitally sign policy to prevent tampering.

2 // Delegated management framework

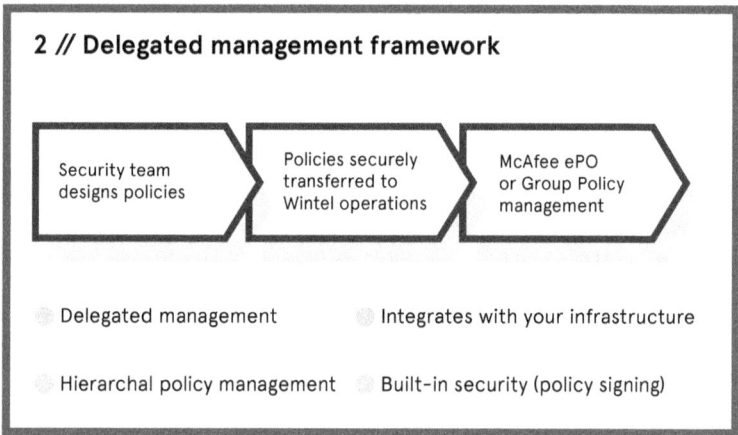

- Delegated management
- Hierarchal policy management
- Integrates with your infrastructure
- Built-in security (policy signing)

 During a deployment of 375K endpoints, IT security ops had the responsibility to create and sanction policy design. However, they had no responsibility to deploy the GPO objects, therefore I needed provisional IT security with the ability to securely create policy and Wintel operations, as well as the ability to deploy. The crucial requirement here was to ensure Wintel operations could not change policy. This was achieved via policy signing.

7.4. Stage 3 – Requirements discovery (understanding your use case)

It's at this point most organisations, project stakeholders and IT professionals will be reduced to quivering wrecks, as they realise they know next to zero about their end user and application estate. I have helped many organisations overcome this in one of two ways. I strongly recommend option 1 for a number of reasons that will become apparent below.

DON'T ASK USERS!

I am not suggesting user communities should not be consulted; of course they should! However, if you ask them a direct question about what access they need the answer you get back will be 'full access' (in other words administrative rights). It is extremely unlikely they will deliver a set of clearly defined use cases.

I would recommend you start by defining a list of job roles or policies. These will range from process worker to innovators; I will discuss this in more detail later in the chapter. This will give you a good starting point to establish the types of use case they will need.

The list below indicates typical use cases that a technical user might require:

- Installing software
- Installing device drivers
- Changing Windows OS settings
- Manually installing updates

DISCOVERY OPTIONS

Consulting with business owners and end user groups will not give you all the answers and consequently you need a solution that will give your organisation insight into what the exact use cases will be. It is extremely important to understand how organisations will initially capture deployment requirements and how these will be translated into design. Therefore, the solution you chose must have the capability to monitor applications and users. A key consideration here is design automation.

Most organisations believe a fully automated approach is required. as this will significantly reduce the deployment time and resource impact. However, in practice this will not work! I strongly recommend against this approach for one simple reason: the only person who fully understands your application landscape is you! With the best will in the world, a fully automated approach will also lead to mis-configured designs – and I have seen this on a number of occasions.

As a result I always recommend a hybrid approach where use cases are captured, analysed and a policy recommendation is provided. It is of the utmost importance that the recommended policy design is ratified by your organisation, tested and then rolled out in phases (starting small and increasing once testing results are positive).

There are two main ways of establishing the use cases. The first deals with requirements from a business logic perspective and the second monitors and discovers the requirements silently.

Both have advantages and disadvantages and in my experience the best way is to leverage a solution that can ultilise business logic to intercept all applications requiring elevation and then prohibit and challenge the user for justification. Trend analysis reports can then be analysed to establish the application requirements.

Alternatively, a silent monitoring mode can be used. This will log applications utilising administrative rights, execute them and log their activity (however, this can lead to false positives when applications have been badly written).

OPTION ONE - APPLICATION INTERCEPTION

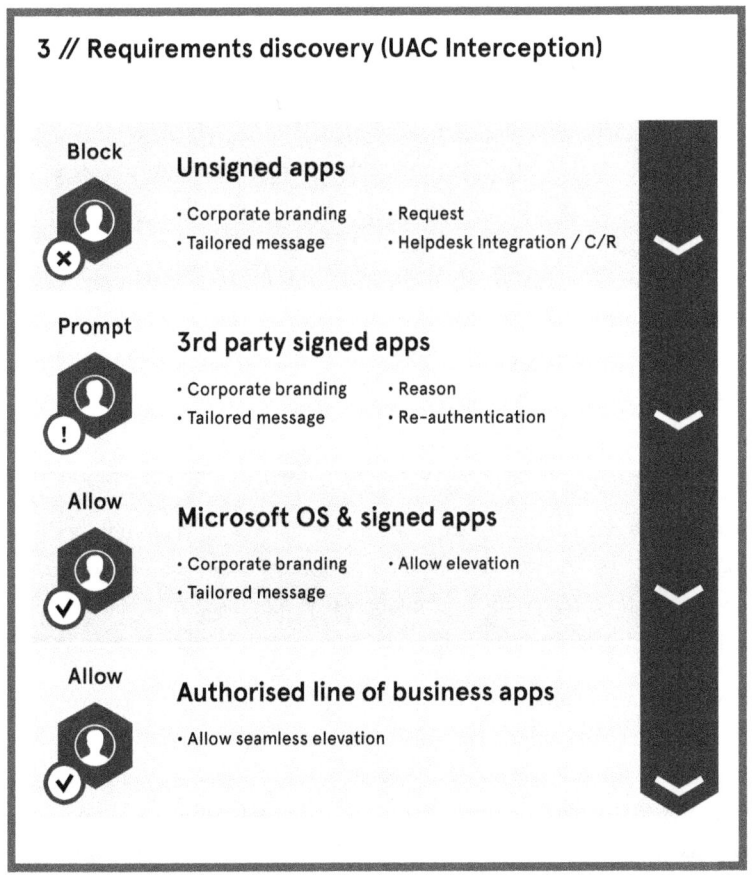

This approach is one of the most effective and quickest to deploy, even within the largest of organisations. Business logic is built into each rule to capture applications requiring elevation, prohibit untrusted applications and sandbox untrusted content. To achieve the above you will need to select a solution with an extensive set of application definition criteria.

The DiD approach described through this book makes this possible. Firstly, you have removed administrative rights and as a result, you can trust key areas for the build, allow applications to run from these locations and prohibit applications running from untrusted locations. This allows application whitelisting to be implemented.

The second step is to incorporate business logic into the rule set that detects applications, tasks, scripts and installers that require administrative rights (triggering UAC) and challenge the user to justify why they need to run them with administrator privileges. Logic can be incorporated to allow benign operating system functions to be elevated by the users, whilst prohibiting them from elevating potentially dangerous or malicious applications. The user can be displayed with a number of different messaging options to ask for justification, re-authentication or unlock codes (I will cover these in more detail later).

Finally, the browsing of untrusted content from external sources will be Sandboxed. This approach is ideal for organisations which have migrated away for XP or server 2003. The key reason for this is that UAC can be leveraged to detect when an application requires administrative rights.

I will provide a worked example below of how I typically set up rules to accommodate this approach. This a theoretical example and would need expanding for production use. I have kept it simple for demonstration purposes. Typically, you would see this style of policy in production once the use cases have been established. However, the level of complexity would need to be increased based upon the roles and needs within your environment.

Rule logic

The important thing to note here is this approach assumes rules are processed in a top down order.

#	Rule Name	Matching Criteria	Description
1	Profile	%userprofile%	Applications running from the user's profile will be prohibited from running and the user will be asked for justification.
2	Unsigned Apps	Wildcard on Publish	Any unsigned and therefore potentially untrusted application will prompt the user before execution.
3	Unsigned Apps requesting Elevated Privileges	Wildcard on Publish + UAC trigger	Any unsigned and therefore potentially untrusted application will prompt the user before execution.
4	MSFT OS functions	%systemroot% + UAC trigger	MSFT operating system functions requiring administrative rights will prompt the user to enter justification prior to being elevated.
5	Trusted locations	%programfiles%	Applications installed in the protected program files location will be allowed to run.

OPTION TWO – SILENT MONITORING

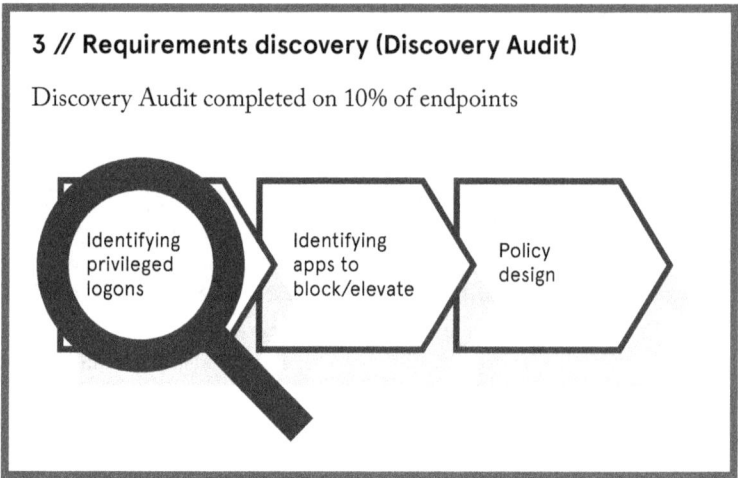

3 // Requirements discovery (Discovery Audit)

Discovery Audit completed on 10% of endpoints

- Identifying privileged logons
- Identifying apps to block/elevate
- Policy design

An alternative to application interception is to silently monitor. Look for a solution that has the capability to be deployed in 'discovery mode', allowing privileged operations and privilege users to be monitored. This should also extend to application launches to establish prohibited applications.

Another key requirement here is the ability to analyse the data discovered. Look for a solution that has enterprise-class data analysis allowing this information to be reviewed and categorised. The information gathered during this stage will be used to provide context to the monitoring data and influence policy design.

The privilege monitoring reports should be detailed, and not only list the applications and privileges they require, but also include the actual privileged operations that were performed, such as access to the registry and file system, and interactions with system services and kernel level objects. Reports should be capable of being automatically generated, detailing the business' user profiles to allow for efficient policy design. In addition to monitoring privileged operations, monitoring of application executions will be required to create whitelist or blacklist applications.

7.5. Stage 4 – Data analysis & use case definition

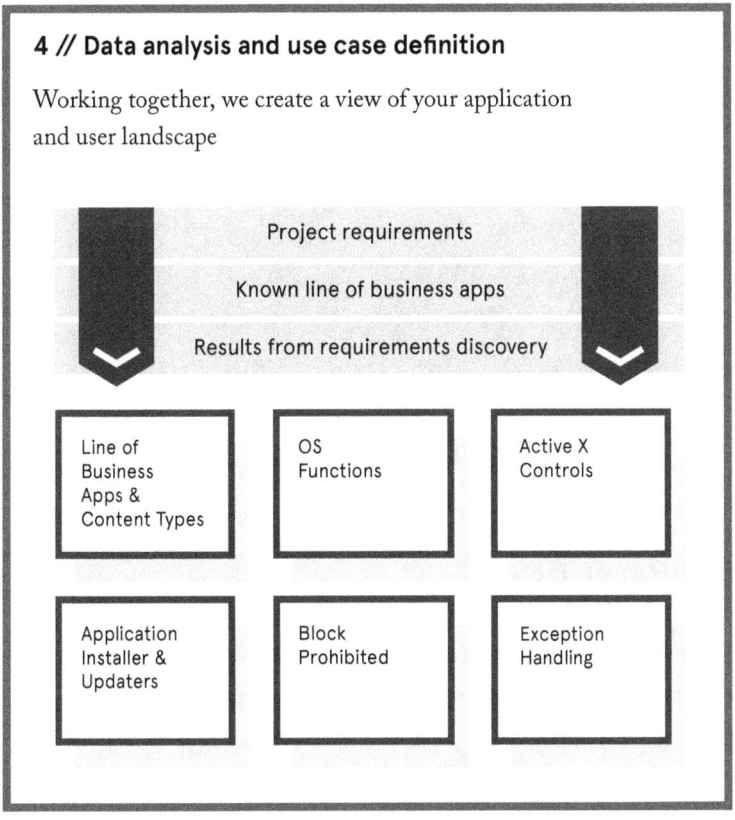

4 // Data analysis and use case definition

Working together, we create a view of your application and user landscape

- Project requirements
- Known line of business apps
- Results from requirements discovery

| Line of Business Apps & Content Types | OS Functions | Active X Controls |
| Application Installer & Updaters | Block Prohibited | Exception Handling |

Once the data has been captured, it is advantageous to have a solution that has the capability to "recommend" a policy design. However, as previously stated, this should always be reviewed by a person who understands the business' needs.

I would recommend a hybrid approach where all of the privileged operations data is analysed in conjunction with the known apps and project requirements. Once the data has been analysed, the tool should provide you with a "recommended" policy design. An example of these recommendations is displayed in the diagram above. This must be ratified by someone who fully understands the business need, rather than being fully automated, which can often lead to policy mis-configuration.

The tooling you select should be capable of incorporating your business logic. For example, if you install all of your business applications to C:\program files\ mycompany and an application which runs from here triggers administrative rights to be utilised then we can assume this is a valid line of business application.

TYPICAL USE CASES

The below list provides an example of use cases that will be established during this stage.

Application elevation

The solution should remove the reliance on local administrator accounts for the execution of applications that require elevated privileges. Instead, an organisation can provide a focused policy to ensure applications will execute under the context of a standard user account. This process allows an application to elevate securely, while conforming to Microsoft best practices.

On-demand privilege elevation

Through integration into the Windows shell menu, the solution should replace the "Run as Administrator" option, providing specific users with the ability to elevate their privileges using an appropriate approval method. This ensures users can gain the access they need for one-off requests, without ever exposing the administrator account or password. Audits and reports on activity provide reports to monitor use.

User Account Control (UAC) replacement

User Account Control is designed to provide a confirmation prompt before an application can make changes to the OS. These prompts are often confusing for end users and can lead to increased demand on helpdesk teams to service their requests. The solution should allow an organisation to harness the UAC trigger and replace standard messages with customised messages that can be configured to block, elevate or audit activity. With complete flexibility of content and branding, the messages provide enhanced communication to improve the end user experience.

Application control

Application control (specifically whitelisting) is recognised as one of the most effective ways of securing a server build, preventing unknown applications from executing. With support for all common forms of script, the solution can secure scripted tasks with strong SHA-1 verification and certificate verification, ensuring that authorised scripts have not been modified or tampered with.

When combined with a privilege management solution that provides the flexibility of an on-demand elevation of privileges, application control can provide all the benefits of a full whitelisting solution, without the administrative overheads.

Application blacklisting

For restricted or unauthorised tasks, a policy can be designed to explicitly block applications or scripts from execution. By using advanced matching criteria, applications can be blocked using any combination of rules, or classifications – such as trusted ownership, or by tracking the origin of where an application was downloaded from. I always advocate Application Control where applicable to whitelist trusted applications and by default, prevent the unknown.

Licence control

When used in conjunction with an application control policy, it is possible to eliminate the installation and execution of unlicenced applications, providing a cost-effective method of controlling or even reducing licence budgets, and ensuring you remain compliant with licence mandates.

Mitigation of "temp admin" processes

When using the on-demand elevation feature within the solution, any existing temporary admin process can be mitigated. A customised confirmation prompt is displayed based on the user's level of access within the organisation. The prompt is extremely flexible and can be configured to include a challenge and response code, over-the-shoulder authentication or self-authentication. In addition, the messages can ask for a reason for the elevation, either through an open text field or pre-populated drop down list.

Prevent rogue admin use

This ensures that users are able to perform effectively with standard user accounts by providing access to the applications, tasks or scripts that have been explicitly stipulated by the solution policy. Any application required outside the predefined list can be executed through an on-demand privilege elevation (appropriate to the user's role), backed by full auditing functionality for full visibility.

Look for a solution that has built in anti-tamper features, which prevent any changes to local privilege groups (including the administrator account/group) to stop any user elevating their privileges. Users are also prevented from changing or altering the solution technology, ensuring the deployment is protected.

Service control

One of the most common administrative tasks performed on servers is the stopping and starting of Windows services. The Windows service type allows individual service operations to be whitelisted, so that standard users are able to start, stop and configure services without the need to elevate tools, such as the Service Control Manager. No modifications are made to any service DACL, keeping the security and integrity of the server build intact.

COM elevation

Embedded within the OS, over 300 User Account Control (UAC) functions require COM elevation. Using the solution, administrators can replace all unwanted UAC prompts with any degree of granularity. Without this feature, tasks such as managing network and advanced network settings, or changing firewall settings would require an administrator account.

Remote PowerShell management

When enabled, Remote PowerShell authorises targeted sysadmins to connect remotely to a computer via WinRM with standard user credentials, which would normally require local administrator rights. Once connected, the sysadmin is then able to execute PowerShell scripts or cmdlets that the solution can elevate, block or audit using a flexible rules engine. This removes the requirement for users to create a terminal connection on a remote machine, which exposes more functionality than may be required to complete the task. Remote PowerShell activity is fully audited, with comprehensive reports.

URL filtering

The solution should track all downloaded applications with the origin URL. These tracked downloads can then be enforced in policy to ensure that only applications from approved or reputable sources are allowed to execute – with all untrustworthy downloads being blocked and audited.

Challenge and response

This feature provides the user with a single use 'challenge' code that requires a matching 'response' approval code. Once the user has the response code from the helpdesk, they are granted access to the application in an audited and controlled manner, even in areas without network connectivity. Applications can be approved by the helpdesk for single use, for the remainder of the sysadmins session, or can be approved on a permanent basis.

Multiple authentication methods can be combined to create a dual authentication process, adding additional security layers to meet compliance requirements.

Delegated Run As

This feature provides a targeted, policy controlled alternative to Windows Run As..., whereby applications and tasks may be executed in the context of a secondary account. The applications where Delegated Run As can be used, by whom, and also the accounts or group of accounts that can be used, are all predetermined by the solution policies.

Advanced policy filtering

The solution's policies should accommodate filters to deal with advanced use cases associated specifically with servers. Filters can be based on Security Group membership, machine or host name, time of day/week, and can be set with a date / time to expire – which can be used in combination with identity management solutions, where provisioned credentials are given a minimal shelf life.

The solution should support Microsoft Remote Desktop Services and Citrix XenApp remote connections, allowing policies to be targeted at remote sessions based on the hostname or IP Address of the remote user. Privileges can then be assigned only to approved remote clients, or through specific routed IP ranges.

A powerful WMI filtering engine allows policies to be targeted at specific server infrastructures using any combination of the thousands of properties available through WMI. For example, policies granting privileged access to IIS administration tools can be targeted at servers with the IIS role.

Discovery of applications

The solution can be placed into a discovery or learning mode to gather information to inform the design of policies. Using its reporting tools, you can identify all applications being executed across the estate. Importantly, you can identify applications requiring administrative rights to execute. This information can then be analysed to build a focused set of policies.

Workflow automation

Look for a solution that can leverage the scripting functionality. An application that is capable of triggering a script can provide instant feedback into existing workflow or management systems. When required, changes to the policies can then be automated through the PowerShell API.

PowerShell API

The solution's PowerShell API provides full policy automation. Administrators can now create and modify the solution policies directly through external workflow management solutions. Through the PowerShell API, you can create and modify any of the solution's configuration within Domain Group Policy, Local Group Policy, or any local configuration.

Enterprise auditing and reporting

Look for a solution that provides enterprise reporting dashboards, leveraging the power of databases such as SQL to provide a breakdown of all user and application privileges. This data can be used to gain a holistic view of all application privileges across the enterprise, including trends in application demand, applications executed outside the core policy and details of user activity.

Patch management/control

Utilising the on-demand privilege elevation feature, you can allow patches and updates to be applied without having to add them to a fixed policy, and importantly, without providing an administrator account. Look for a solution that can automate this via a PowerShell API to create/modify policy on a targeted set of machines and authorise the update under specific conditions.

7.6. Stage 5 – Layering policies

The work carried out in stage 4 will allow you to establish your policy framework and answer the design questions establish so far. This insight is vital for ensuring that your policy design meets your exact objectives and requirements.

THE ENDPOINT SECURITY PARADOX

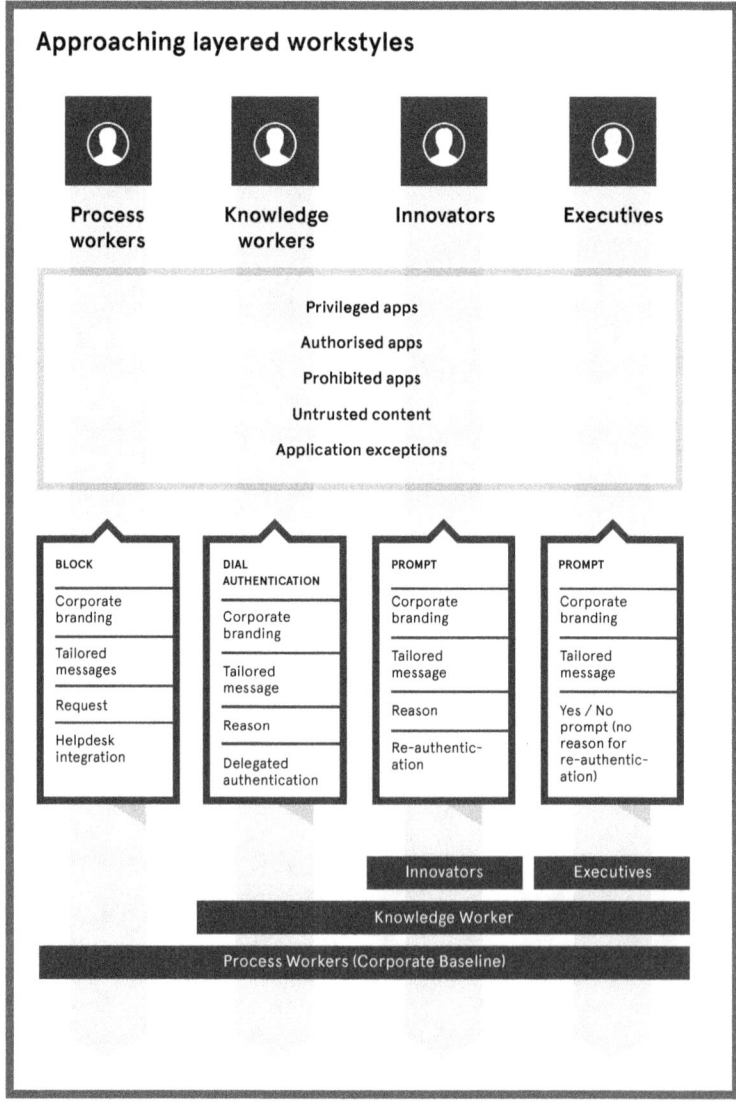

Enabling the production of layered policies is of key importance. Policy layering enables you to dramatically reduce the total cost of ownership (TOC) of the solution and ensures that your build remains clean, simple and scalable. Utilising the solution across all endpoints, organisations are able to create rules for all user profiles within the environment. Once logged in with standard user rights, the policy applied will allow elevation, application whitelisting and sandboxing based on the user roles and requirements.

A powerful filtering engine ensures that a specific policy can be assigned to different environments. Policies can be assigned to individual users, or groups, and can be time-bound so they are only effective during scheduled maintenance windows. Advanced filtering using WMI allows focused delivery of use case only to endpoints and profiles that need it. Policies can also offer levels of flexibility based on job description or seniority, where process workers and external contractors are given tighter, more regulated restrictions than more senior roles.

Look for a solution with a wide range of filtering options available. This will help ensure individuals or teams can be managed based on role, job function or even specific tasks, rather than as a one-size-fits-all.

The key here is that the policies will be aggregated together, building on the previous layer. For example, the process worker's policy would be deployed across the estate, as a baseline, with the other polices layered on top. Most users will fall into the Knowledge and Innovators category, which will build on top of the process worker's policy (or in other words corporate base line).

The next challenge is all about how you deal with exceptions. Exception handling options are required to ensure that applications, operating system functions, tasks, scripts and installations are only restricted for valid reasons. Anyone having a valid business reason to use/install a restricted item will have the option of requesting access when prompted. This can be achieved by implementing challenge and response functionality, whereby a request is sent to the IT helpdesk for a secure 8-digit code to gain the access they need. This is all within the context of a standard user account. The entire process can be automated with ticketing systems, and email / web alerts, as well as customised with corporate branding and text. This ensures a rich and intuitive user experience, without heavy resource requirements.

 The key is not to get in the way of the user's ability to do his/her job. Choose the solution that provides the most comprehensive set of exception handling options, which we'll look at next.

Example policies

A junior sysadmin needs access to perform some low level maintenance tasks, such as check/clear event logs, defragment and cleanup disks, etc. administrative rights to these specific tasks is granted during out-of-hours only.

A security engineer needs access to manage the server's firewall configuration. Privileged access to the Windows firewall control panel, as well the ability to restart *only* the Windows firewall service is granted.

An external consultant needs access to manage the configuration of a VOIP server. Privileged access is granted to only the VOIP management tools and the VOIP service.

A senior sysadmin needs to diagnose a server outage, and requires access to the server to diagnose the issue. A flexible 'on demand' policy is assigned, allowing the sysadmin privileged and audited access to core Windows' debugging tools. Access to Windows services is gated with Challenge/Response, requiring authorisation from a support desk.

A maintenance engineer needs to install a patch/hotfix on a server. Privileges are assigned to run the specific patch MSP only.

EXCEPTION HANDLING

6 // Exception handling

- Automatic suppression of UAC and seamless elevation
- Seamless sandboxing of untrusted sites and content
- Comprehensive end user messaging to handle Exceptions
    - » Corporate branding
    - » Full text configuration and localization
    - » Reason/request entry
    - » Helpdesk Integration (hyperlink or email)
    - » Password and smartcard authentication
    - » Challenge/response mechanism
    - » Over the shoulder administration

As discussed, scenarios will arise where exceptions need to be made and the users are able to request access to functionality outside of their defined policy e.g. a mobile worker needs to install software off-site. Exception handling ensures you have a strategy for dealing with the grey area and it's key to ensuring the balance between security and user freedom by providing users with the options to easily request access to any unknown applications. This provides IT and security teams with the control and visibility they need to ensure security, while empowering users to be productive in their day-today job roles.

A flexible policy design platform is required, whereby different user profiles/polices can be created to match the varying needs of different groups of users e.g. task based worker, mobile worker, Power User. Policies and their rules can be stacked/ordered so that resultant sets of policies apply varying levels of controls to different polices. Applications can then be grouped together based on different user demands, further simplifying policy design.

These exceptions need to be catered for in various ways i.e:

- **Challenge & response**, where a customisable message will be displayed providing a challenge code for which a response code is needed to proceed. The response code can be communicated to the user by text message, URL or by helpdesk integration. The solution recommends a series of questions before granting the response code to ensure the user needs the application for a valid business purpose.
- **Ticketing request**, following a customisable message or application launch, a helpdesk ticket could be automatically logged. The solution includes a very powerful and flexible scripting engine, which has been designed to allow integration into an organisation's existing infrastructure.
- **Email request**, where a customisable message will be displayed and prompt the user for information, which can be submitted by email to the responsible IT team/manager.

- **URL request**, where a customisable message will be displayed and direct the user to a URL requesting information that can be submitted to the responsible IT team/manager.

- **Support authorisation**, where a customisable message displayed requires an authorised user to type in their credentials so that the user may proceed.

 In my experience, well developed policies should be able to deal with 80 to 85% of cases the user encounters. The remaining 15 to 20% will be dealt with via exception handling and therefore this plays a crucial role in the success of your project.

QUICK WINS – A LAYER AT A TIME

As the saying goes, "Rome was not built in a day"; it was built a layer at a time! What I mean by this is that many of my clients have found it much easier to deploy a defence layer one at a time. For example, many organisations will deploy sandboxing (with built in app control) as a quick win, in the first instance. This allows a layer of protection to be deployed quickly with minimal configuration effort.

I would then recommend deploying privilege management, thus allowing you to take back control of the endpoint. The final layer should then be application whitelisting. You need to be in control of the endpoint prior to rolling out application control, otherwise you cannot be confident your trusted location rules are secure.

7.7. Stage 6 – Policy testing

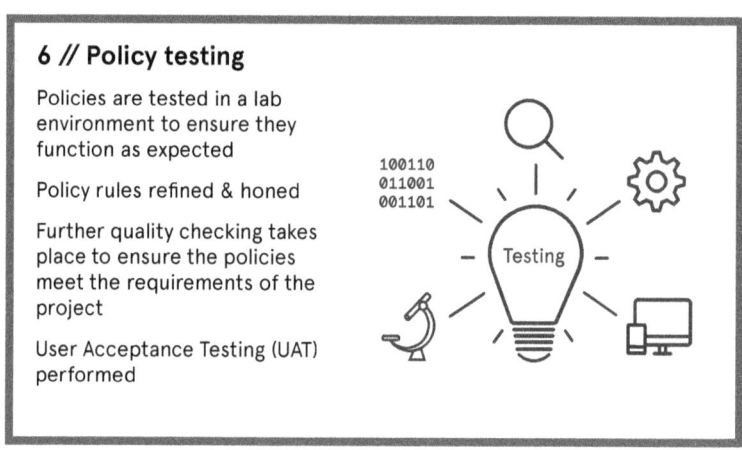

6 // Policy testing

Policies are tested in a lab environment to ensure they function as expected

Policy rules refined & honed

Further quality checking takes place to ensure the policies meet the requirements of the project

User Acceptance Testing (UAT) performed

It is of the utmost importance that the recommended policy design is ratified by your organisation, tested and then rolled out in a phases (starting small and increasing once UAT testing results are positive). Regardless of the size of your enterprise you should start small. I have worked with some of the largest organisations on the planet and had to reset expectations on the testing sizes so be prepared to go smaller than you'd expect.

PILOT PHASING

The implementation of DiD within your organisation should begin with a pilot. This must consist of users from different business units. If your organisation is standardised on a single OS, has little to no variance in configuration, and has a very controlled and predictable environment, a pilot may not be necessary. However, most organisations will perform some sort of pilot and this should align to project goals and objectives to ensure they are met.

WORKSHEET

The following list provides some example test criteria:	
Technical and operational infrastructure integration	
How to roll-out the software to endpoints	
Refine project requirements	
Establish how best to communicate with end users	
Refine the goals and objectives	
Establish how to communicate the outcome to users and management	
Installation - time and complexity	
Usage - ease of use, completeness of solution in regards to requirements	
Overall experience, product and vendor	
Establish rule review criteria, process and responsibilities that mimic actual teams involved in day-to-day operations.	

End users must have communication validation	
Determine integration with existing change control procedures and policies.	
Determine the team responsible for implementation and ongoing support.	
Establish procedures for coordinating efforts between team members.	
Validate that the test environment is fully functional	
Test users from multiple groups within the organisation	
Aim to test 40% to 60% of use cases built into policies	
Perform co-exist testing	
Run User Acceptance Testing feedback sessions, which will lead into policy tweaking	

The users selected for the pilot will have the solution deployed to their machines in order to ensure the correct balance has been struck between security and freedom. This will involve the removal of local administrative rights, and the addition of Application Control and Sandboxing. Each user in the pilot group should work as normal to ensure that all approved and necessary applications and processes are working properly.

It is recommended that all test users are allowed to work for at least a couple of weeks to ensure that all normal day-to-day applications and processes have been identified. Any instances where users experience problems can be addressed quickly and polices adjusted accordingly.

The size and duration of the pilot will need to be determined by the project team and should align to your organisation's process and procedures. The pilot should not be longer than it needs to be but needs to be long enough to allow issues to be established. I routinely see pilots lasting around a month. The Pilot must demonstrate how the solution can be used to improve the security posture and operational efficiencies within an environment.

I would recommend running a pilot that looks like the following:

- **Has multiple departments**
- **Custom or industry applications**
- **Supports multiple versions of Windows desktops and servers**
- **Large help desks to support a diverse environment**

7.8. Stage 7 – Internal communication

> ### 7 // Internal announcements
>
> Internal comms templates provided based on our past experience
>
> We will advise on a best practice approach to manage change
>
> Users positively accept change if well communicated
>
> T-minus style communications keep users updated

The political and cultural challenges of implementing DiD can be hard to overcome, if not tackled in the correct way. I cannot stress enough how important this stage is to the success of your project. This and this alone could be the downfall of the project. Consequently, I place a significant emphasis on user education and communication.

It is expected that users will accept change if it is communicated well, allowing them to understand the benefits. This will help minimise helpdesk support incidents related to the removal of elevated rights. It's also important to set up a feedback mechanism (e.g. intranet, email, nominated contact) for questions and answers.

Although this is the first time I have talked about end user communication in detail, it is important to note that there may be multiple communication stages within a project, and so I recommend reviewing where in the project plan this should fit and choose the optimal place for your environment.

USER PUSH BACK!

You should be prepared for users to push back once administrative rights are removed and application control is put in place. In addition, do not be surprised if you lose the backing of management when faced with an unhappy workforce. I have seen so many security projects fail when security gets in the way of a user's ability to do their job. Users may feel that such measures are draconian and that they are not trusted.

The larger the organisation, the more likely such projects will be supported and seen as normal and I would expect less push back.

USER ACCEPTANCE – SECURITY SHOULD BE SEEN AS AN ENABLER

Crucially user acceptance comes down to presenting the changes in a positive light. Users are more likely to accept change if they understand it and feel they are gaining. Security should be an enabler. It is important to make sure you not only communicate how their computing experience will change and improve, but also explain the benefits for the company.

Well-designed DiD strategy allows users to fulfil their responsibilities without being exposed to unnecessary risks and maintains performance and reliability. Information and systems security is in the interests of the company, ensuring it can remain competitive.

DID IS FOR EVERYONE – THAT INCLUDES EXECUTIVES

I have discussed the importance of management buy-in already, but it is also important that managers set an example and are part of the project themselves. Too often, managers decide to exclude themselves on the basis that they are a part of management. If managers don't think a scheme is important, neither will the employees.

LANGUAGE CAN BE YOUR DOWNFALL!

The language used to promote the project should be positive and it is best to avoid using language such as 'lockdown' and 'restricted privileges'. Such terms do not sit well with users, and create the feeling that draconian controls are being put in place. If users can no longer perform a particular task on their endpoint, be ready to provide some justification.

END USERS ARE NOT IDIOTS!

Explain the WHY! Users will be more receptive to the project if they understand why you are implementing DiD. Explain the thought processes and how the decisions have been made. Mentioning the security aspects directly should be avoided. Failure to communicate creates an environment of suspicion and control. It is important that users understand why IT is trying to secure the environment and how this will help their job roles.

 I have seen projects fail when they have not been communicated effectively and the policy design has been dictated to end users. In fact, I've seen the solution deployed to 10,000 machines WITHOUT any policy testing and this ultimately failed, as the DiD policies could not provide the correct level of elevation.

 I have worked with an engineering organisation which had all the right intentions but failed to communicate with the end users and gather requirements. Instead they imposed policy on them. In addition there was no feedback mechanism. This ultimately led to failure.

SECURITY WORKSHOPS

Education helps to establish trust and get users on-side. They will be more aware of why security initiatives are important, how they are relevant to their own roles, and how security issues affect the business' profit if security workshops are run.

7.9. Stage 8 – Production deployment

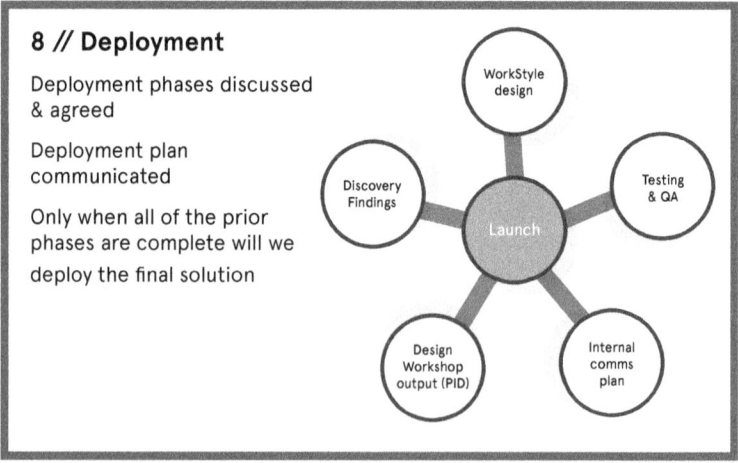

Although we have covered a lot of ground by this point in the project, we still have a lot of decisions to make. For example, deployment phases, UAT period and rollout plans. Now the pilot is complete, the remaining corporate user base will be ready for deployment. This will be a phased rollout, with the phases based around:

- Site
- Department/business-unit
- Geographical location
- User role
- Asset type
- Network architecture considerations
- Your business needs and implementation plan
- OS versions

Consideration must be given to the existing architecture of the endpoints and the overall network. I would recommend grouping similar assets (desktops and servers) and locations together, as this will ensure the experiences are similar and you are not dealing with multiple problems should they arise.

Also, consider future OS changes and the overall technology. Do the OS and policies applied need to be altered due to OS version?

Think about geographical location. If engineering is located in every physical building and location, including all engineering desktops in one phase might not be the ideal solution. Instead, organising the desktops per location or city might be a better approach.

I would recommend looking for existing deployment methodologies within your organisation and aligning to those. For example, logical groupings may align with existing Active Directory Organisation Units (OU) and may be the best guidance for managing the implementation by group.

PLANNING

Planning and execution is the key to a successful implementation. Analysis of the pilot results will feed into the production rollout plan and help the refinement of goals and objectives. This will allow the production release plan to be updated easily. If the pilot has flagged up issues with either the technology or the planning, you need to review the approach to production implementation. The following are examples of areas that can cause problems and ultimately delay the deployment process:

- No clearly defined success criteria
- Unrealistic schedule for deployment (i.e. rushed rollout)
- Lack of commitment or user involvement from the defined functional groups
- Changes in the project leadership before completion
- Production system images and applications not included in the pilot group
- Exceptions handling is not correct set up

During the pilot it is extremely important to document any challenges that occurred and the resolution(s). These could be related to a number of areas, including technology, internal change control procedures and support staff requirements. Use this information to refine the remaining project stage as the solution is deployed across the enterprise. These may result in some stages being replayed, such as the policy design stages. This will diminish over time.

DEPLOYMENT SCHEDULE

Week	Task
1	Deploy the policy to 50 machines and gather feedback
2	Meet to discuss feedback and make any tweaks / changes required. Also re-test
3	Increase the coverage of the policy to 100 machines
4	Meet to discuss feedback and make any tweaks / changes required. Also re-test
5	Increase the coverage of the policy to 200 machines
6	Meet to discuss feedback and make any tweaks / changes required. Also re-test
7 - x	Keep doubling deployment numbers and tweaking until your reach 1000 machines
8	It is common at this point to factor some time in here for knowledge transfer and possible helpdesk training
9	In larger environments, it is recommended to run the solution over a number of weeks, increasing the coverage of the policy so that one global site gets complete coverage. In this case I would normally recommend that this site be one that is geographically close to (in the same time zone) as the main point of contacts for the support of the solution
10-x	Once 1,000 machines have been reached, the rollout starts to hit larger quantities. Continue to increase the policy to cover extra business units / global sites until we have reached all machines / users in scope for the production policy

REMOVING ADMINISTRATIVE RIGHTS

There are many ways to remove administrative rights; typically, I recommend one of the following:

- **Restricted Users and Groups GPO:** This can be used to wipe and reapply group settings or append.
- **Local Users and Groups Extension (Preferences):** Group Policy includes the Local Users and Groups preference extension. This extension allows you to centrally manage local users and groups on domain member computers.

Other common methods include startup scripts and SCCM configuration tasks. I would recommend performing some research and testing these out in a lab environment prior to production rollout. It is also important to understand how rights are granted in the first place. I have seen organisations remove administrative rights only to find higher precedence GPOs reapply them.

When I delivered 100k seats to a defence contractor in the US, we aligned the provisioning of policy with the expiry of the existing admin account process. Users had to request administrative rights periodically, and on expiry they would be provisioned into the correct policy group within AD. This simplified the process and allowed for touch points with the end users.

7.10. STAGE 9 – BUSINESS AS USUAL SUPPORT (POST DEPLOYMENT)

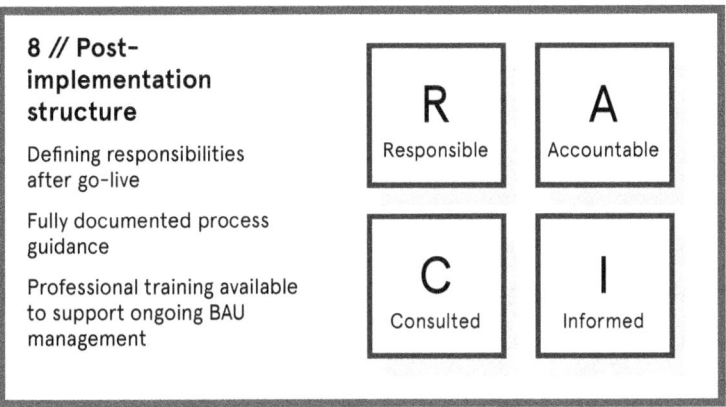

After deployment there is still work to be done, in the form of ensuring you have established post deployment ownership. In my experience, many organisations often overlook the importance of deciding post-implementation project structure. It is important to ensure the areas of responsibilities are defined so that you have the structure in place to refine and adapt the polices as the needs of your organisation evolve. Once established I would recommend setting up a business as usual handover procedure to ensure that teams managing the solution fully accept their areas of ownership. This should include product and process training.

 You need a product that will grow with you and not be restrictive.

I generally recommend my clients build a RACI (Roles, Accountable, Consulted, Informed) matrix, as shown in the slide above. Although this is discussed at stage 9, this really should be built throughout the life of the project.

I've seen deployment teams disbanded after deployment and administrative rights being given back because people don't understand or are not aware a tool is in place.

SETTING EXPECTATIONS

All DiD projects will require post-implementation attention for new applications and environmental changes. Procedures need to be developed on how these new applications will be monitored, discovered, and solved. This includes bringing in various teams to report on the change and implement the solution.

Expectations will need to be set to ensure users do not place unreasonable demands on the teams owning the solutions. Creating a catalogue of services that your IT department offers helps to set expectations. Service catalogues show the business how IT services align to business needs, establishing trust between IT and the business, by showing the value of services.

SUPPORT SERVICE LEVEL AGREEMENTS (SLA)

Ensure you set both internal and external SLAs. Internal SLAs can be documented in the service catalogues. If the product vendor needs to be involved, ensure that the vendor has SLAs that meet your needs and is available when you need it. For example 24/7/365 support for all products and technologies included in the solution.

KNOWLEDGE TRANSFER

It is impossible to expect the solution owners to get the best out of it, if they have not had training. Team members need to be trained on the various aspects of the solution, including communication, training and labs for testing any in-project items. The solution and the different components also need to be documented. This would typically be built up through the life of the project and handed over at the end as an "as built" document.

Typical items include:

- Policy deployment architecture
- Reporting architecture
- Agent deployment architecture
- Delegation of control models used
- Policy and rule logical
- New policy, rule and definition creation

CHAPTER 8
Building group consensus

By now you will be able to see how success can be achieved. However, before you start a project like this there is one more challenge to overcome – group consensus. In the face of large and complex organisations, with multiple decision makers this can be a challenge I have seen many organisations settle for what is essentially weak security because they simply struggled to agree on anything else. Without consensus the project may never see the light of day.

I have helped many business leaders and technical stakeholder navigate the process of consensus building and that is what I want to focus on here. I have broken the process of consensus building into four stages. The focus here is to help establish your business objectives and not to build a project delivery team (that is covered in chapter 7).

Stage one – Understanding group conflict

If one thing is certain – there will be group conflict! You should not shy away from this; instead front this up as early in the process as possible. Try to understand the viewpoints of all stakeholders and clearly document the issues facing them and their teams. Do not wait until later in the project in the hope that the issues will go away. This approach runs a greater risk of completely de-railing the project and resulting in failure.

Once you understand the pain points, bring suppliers in earlier than you would typically aim to. Studies have shown that group conflict peaks at

37% yet project stakeholders do not seek external advice until they are 57% certain the project will work. Think about this for a moment – how many projects have failed before they have even started?

Stage two – Build the team

Understand who the key decision makers are in the process and involve them from the start. Do not leave out potential road blockers (if they should be involved), as they will only put the project at risk after a large amount of effort has been put in. There are typically 5.4 decision makers involved in enterprise projects and the more people involved, the less likely the project will be a success.. Do not be fooled into thinking people can be left out of the decision making process. Not including them will only have detrimental effects further down the line.

The key here is to understand the traits of the individuals in the team. This will allow you to play to their strengths, whilst mitigating any issues they may cause. Look for people that exhibit the following traits:

- Champions good ideas
- Always delivers more than asked
- Learns from mistakes and does not repeat
- Often teaches insights to colleagues
- Colleagues and senior executives seek their advice
- Good at convincing others
- Perceives unclear projects as risky and wants to clarify
- Prepares influential stakeholders for disruptive ideas
- Believes changes require small wins first which build over time

My experienced has shown that focusing on people that exhibit the above traits creates a recipe for success. Typically, you would not find someone that holds skills in all of the above areas, so try to bring a team together that blends the above.

Stage three – Confronting group conflict

Setup workshops to discover the pain points, business objectives, requirements and success criteria for the project. Look for consultants and vendors who can offer technology agnostic workshops, which can help you, navigate the conflicts and come up with workable solutions. Search for insight into the scope of any consultancy effort, for both Proof of Concepts (PoCs) and production deployment. If members of the team are being prohibitive, try to brake-down their mental models, which are stopping group consensus being agreed upon and address each issue head on. Use the workshops for this and look to consultants and vendors to provide insight as to when and how they have solved these issues before. Avoid vendors who lack real world experience.

Focusing on the following areas early will help identify issues, without waiting until substantial work has been conducted. The aim for the workshop should be to identify and measure points of conflict. Encourage the exchange of views, especially if conflicting – this helps you breakdown objections should they arise. The list below will ultimately lead to clear project success criteria.

- Discuss priorities/needs and highlight differences
- Uncover subtle/unexpected implications
- Uncover unvoiced concerns
- Identify benefits of the right solution
- Identify consequences and costs of not acting
- Ask influencers to share why others are supporting the project
- Drive debate into the "too hard" or "too stressful" areas
- What do we not know but should?
- What are we missing?
- Focus on getting things right vs just getting things done

 **WORKSHEET**

Running a workshop

Prepare	
Clear purpose and agenda - and start on time	

Manage	
Restate purpose and agenda at the start	
Control interruptions	
Protect the shy and quiet	
Contain the noisy	
Control discussions that wander off the point	
Stop "meetings within meetings"	
Accept differences of opinion – but contain conflict between individuals – keep to business issues	
Ensure everyone is involved and contributing	
Record points of view – I often use a flip chart for this – that way everyone can see the recorded items.	

Close	
Call a halt: Remind everyone of goals and objectives	
Summarise input from all sides	
Agree next steps	
Finish on time	
Follow up	
Document outcome and actions asap and distribute	

CHAPTER 9
Tools and vendor selection

9.1.	Security	194
9.2.	Features	195
9.3.	Ease of use	196
9.4.	Architecture	197
9.5.	Support	198
9.6.	Innovation	198
9.7.	Vendor selection questions	199

Forrester's 'Endpoint Security Trends, Q2 2013 to Q4 2014' report showed that 60% of enterprises prefer to source their solutions from a single vendor as it can lower the administrative burden. "Investing in product suites allows S&R pros to take advantage of suite discounting while acquiring a broader set of security technologies. Ancillary benefits include less time spent training security staff on multiple interfaces while giving security pros integrated management and reporting for a better overall security posture."

With the above in mind I want to set out key criteria which should be looked at when choosing a vendor. These do not only apply to DiD projects but can be used generally for I.T. projects. The order the criteria are presented here is important.

9.1. Security

Security needs to be built in to the solution from the ground up and not retro fitted or applied over the top, as this will inherently lead to weakness in the solution. Consider the solution against the following:

- **Protect the integrity of the solution:** The solution must be intelligent enough to protect itself, with in-built security measures. Users/malware must not be able to leverage elevated processes to disable or tamper with the components of the solution.
- **Local system protection:** The solution must prevent the manipulation of privileged user account groups.
- **Malware attack vector protection:** The solution must offer protection against common malware attack vectors, including code injections, shatter attacks and token hijacks.
- **Policy authenticity:** The solution should include the option for policies to be controlled, only allowing the right people to author and distribute.
- **Multi-layered management delegation:** The solution must provide a delegation management platform, therefore allowing disparate teams to manage key aspects of the solution.
- **Proactive prevention:** The solution must allow you to establish and define what trusted software within your environment is. This secures endpoints by preventing untrusted software, such as advanced and targeted threats, from executing in your environment.
- **Complements existing security solutions:** The solution should integrate with existing tools and not prohibit them from functioning.
- **Granular control of administrative rights:** Make sure the solution can design and build security that can apply targeted administrative rights without having to over-privilege applications and users.

9.2. Features

You should consider the future and what requirements your organisation will have 12 months into the deployment. I have seen organisations choose solutions based on price, only to find it could not cope with additional demand placed on it further down the line.

- **Process elevation:** Ensure that administrative rights can be assigned to individual applications, tasks and scripts without requiring the user to be granted full administrative rights, along with the ability to create custom privilege tokens.
- **Diverse application support:** The solution must provide broad application support, including native support of hosted file types, such as Control Panel Applets (.cpl) and Microsoft Management Consoles (.msc).
- **Board application identification:** The solution must support a broad and varied range of application identification criteria that are consistent across the tooling and provide the ability to combine multiple criteria together.
- **Application whitelisting:** Prevent the execution of unauthorised applications through a combination of user-centric application whitelisting and blacklisting.
- **Zero Day protection:** Protect trusted applications (i.e. office) from web-borne threats that gain access to the users' data.
- **Identify privilege requirements:** Detect and audit which users, applications, installers, tasks and scripts require administrative rights.
- **Auditing and reporting:** Provide application trend analysis, including which applications are being run, by which user and on which machines.

9.3. Ease of use

The solution should start simple and stay simple regardless of size of the deployment.

- **Easy to implement and maintain:** Policy design should be consistent and clear throughout the solution.
- **Layered policies:** Policies should be created to align with the roles and responsibilities within your organisation. This allows policies to be layered, providing the ability to aggregate privileges and function together.
- **Custom messaging:** Effective communication with users should be central to this solution. Communication via customisable, corporately branded, end user messaging will replace confusing and unintuitive system messages and therefore ensure flexibility and successful user adoption.
- **Request workflow:** The solution should provide a mechanism to allow the user to gain access to applications after providing justification and optional re-authentication to ensure a positive user experience, while supporting tracking and auditing requirements.
- **Fully replace User Account Control (UAC) messages:** By overriding UAC users have a mechanism to request access, with clear and concise messages that result in a superior end user experience.
- **Minimal user impact:** The solution should be hassle-free for the end user.

9.4. Architecture

The solution must be capable of leveraging existing infrastructure and not reinvent the wheel, as this adds delay and cost.

- **Integration with existing technologies:** The solution must build on existing technologies such as Active Directory or McAfee ePO
- **Reporting platform:** The reporting capabilities must be able to consolidate audit data into the existing central server that can correlate events over time by leveraging existing technologies.
- **Single agent:** Maintaining a lightweight core image is important and therefore all features of the solution must be controlled through a single client-side agent that does not have a material impact on the performance of the endpoints.
- **Single management console:** Ongoing maintenance should be performed from a single point of administration and must not place significant strain on internal resources.
- **Centrally managed policy:** The solution must provide a central mechanism for policies to be deployed.
- **Policy automation:** The solution must provide the ability to automate the creation and deployment of policies, through technologies such as PowerShell.
- **Comprehensive platform coverage:** The solution must cover all platforms equally providing feature parity regardless of OS version or deployment technology used.
- **Scalability:** The solution must be capable of scaling to support hundreds of thousands of endpoints.

9.5. Support

- **Global support:** The vendor must provide a support operation covering 24 hours, 365 days a year, with access to local engineers and online ticketing for raising and tracking support cases
- **Professional services:** The solution must be accompanied by a professional services consultancy to aid with design and implementation. This is crucial to ensure project success and will support the handover of the solution to Business As Usual (BAU) operations.
- **Implementation methodology:** There must be a proven and robust implementation methodology surrounding the solution, based upon successful project deployments. This enables you to maximise investment and ensure the software deployment meets the defined requirements

9.6. Innovation

Any vendor can say they are innovators or are going to innovate, but you can only judge them on their past performance and the proof is in the numbers. Look for a vendor that has consistently innovated and pushed the boundaries of what endpoint security software can do. Compare feature release notes to see which vendors have brought features to the market first.

TOOLS AND VENDOR SELECTION

 **WORKSHEET**

9.7. Vendor selection questions

I have put together a set of questions which will help you in the event your organisation has to build a tender:

Architecture and management	
1. What infrastructure is required to support the management of the solution?	
2. What platforms are supported for the management components of the solution?	
3. Is the solution integrated with Active Directory Group Policy?	
4. Does the solution support offline users?	
5. Does the solution support integration into the McAfee ePO Framework?	
6. Does the solution support delegated administration?	
7. Does the solution support computer and/or user configurations?	

8. Does the solution obey Group Policy precedence rules when applying multiple GPOs?	
9. Does the solution support Resultant Set of Policy (RSoP)?	
10. Does the solution support Advanced Group Policy Management (AGPM) and other third party Group Policy change control products?	
11. What automation options does your solution provide?	

Privilege Management

1. Does the solution allow users to work under standard user accounts?	
2. Does the solution support the seamless elevation of individual applications?	
3. Does the solution support advanced users, who may need to elevate applications on demand?	
4. What types of application can the solution manage?	

5. Does the solution provide application templates for built-in operating system tasks and common third party applications?	
6. Can applications be grouped together to simplify management?	
7. Can policies be created that target different users and/or computers?	
8. Can temporary policies be created with expiry times?	
9. Does the solution include built-in security tokens to grant administrative rights to users?	
10. Does the solution allow granular security tokens to be defined?	
11. Can the inheritance of privileges by child processes be controlled?	
12. Does the solution secure file open save dialogs within elevated applications?	
13. Does the solution support the discovery of privileged applications before administrative rights are removed from users?	

14. Can the solution suppress or replace ALL UAC consent dialogs?	
15. Does your solution support the remote management of machines and servers?	
16. How are you going to provide different day-to-day functions for different job roles?	
17. What support do you provide for Windows 8.1 applications and how do you deal with exceptions?	
18. How does your solution deal with application installs coming from external sources, such as the internet?	

End user experience

1. Does the solution allow a custom message to be displayed before an application is launched or blocked?	
2. Can multiple messages be defined?	
3. Is the message text fully configurable? Is multi-lingual support included?	
4. Can an optional reason/request be included in a custom message?	

5. Can the user be forced to re-authenticate before launching an application?	
6. Can the messages be branded, for instance with a corporate logo or banner?	
7. How are you going to handle messaging your multi-regional workforce?	
8. What exception handling capabilities exist in your application to deal with applications not defined in policy?	

Application control

1. Does the solution provide application control capabilities	
2. Does the solution support blacklisting and whitelisting simultaneously?	
3. Does the solution support exception handling from restricted and unknown applications?	
4. What types of applications can be controlled?	
5. Does the solution support granular control of child process for black or whitelisting?	

Agent	
1. Does the solution require an agent to be installed on the endpoint?	
2. What platforms are supported by the agent?	
3. How is the agent packaged?	
4. Is the agent upgradable?	
5. How does the agent protect its integrity?	
6. What performance impact does the agent have on the system?	
7. Are policies cached and still applied when the endpoint is not connected to the corporate network?	
8. How are cached policies secured?	

Security of solution	
1. Does your solution protect the admin group from modification?	
2. Does your solution prevent users overriding the system from an elevated process?	
3. Does your solution identify privilege logons?	
4. Can you prevent execution of unwanted child processes from an elevated application?	
5. Can you allow the installation of applications to be executed securely from a trusted source, such as a URL? (app store etc)	
6. Can your solution provide granular, secure control for services?	
7. How does your solution protect the elevated application from malware attacks?	

Security of data in cloud platforms	
1. Do you have processes and procedures around physical access to the servers that host client data?	
2. How do you vet employees with access to client data?	
3. Is the environment shared or true multi-tenant? If shared, is the data guaranteed to be secure from other organisations?	
4. If another customer was to overuse the environment could it impact my solution?	
5. How is data secured during transmission from the client to the server environment?	
6. Do you maintain full audit trails of access to the environment?	
7. Which country is the data stored in? Do you guarantee it will never leave that country?	

Auditing and reporting	
1. What centralised reporting capabilities are available with the solution?	
2. What platforms are supported for reporting?	
3. What preconfigured dashboards and reports are included?	
4. Can custom reports be created?	
5. What events are audited?	
6. What information is audited in these events?	
7. Is there granular control over the raising of events?	
8. Does your solution identify the applications that require admin rights or that you want to block?	
9. Does your solution provide details of why an application needs administrative rights to run?	
10. What trend analysis does your solution provide?	
11. How does the solution analyse and provide policy recommendations?	

Implementation and training	
1. What is the largest implementation of your solution?	
2. Please describe the phases of a typical implementation?	
3. Does your company offer an official training course? Support and maintenance?	
4. What are your standard hours of support?	
5. Do you offer 24/7 support?	
6. What are your support response times?	
7. Do you provide a standard Service Level Agreement?	
8. What methods are available for engaging with your support function?	
9. Do you have an online knowledgebase?	
10. Please provide insight into your support statistics and customer satisfaction?	
11. What tools are provided to troubleshoot your solution?	

TOOLS AND VENDOR SELECTION

Sandboxing	
1. Does the solution offer a sandbox module?	
2. What operating systems does the sandbox support?	
3. Does the sandbox have a separate management platform?	
4. Does the sandbox rely on heuristics for detection?	
5. Does the sandbox require any additional infrastructure?	
6. Does the sandbox use virtualisation for isolating potential threats?	
7. Does the sandbox require network connectivity for threat behaviour detection?	
8. What applications and content does the sandbox support?	
9. Does the sandbox support application updates and new versions out of the box?	
10. How does the solution protect against zero day vulnerabilities in known, trusted applications?	

CHAPTER 10
Final thoughts

Securing your endpoints does not have to be hard but I constantly see history repeating itself. The irony is you do not need to be a security expert to protect your environment: you just need to build your environment on solid foundations. There are so many misconceptions about effectiveness and so much hype, I can see why the same attack vectors are exploited.

However, because of the range of implications, cyber security cannot be left entirely to the IT and security teams. Ultimately, the board will be held accountable if a company falls victim to a cyber attack and in many cases, they may be held personally liable. Everyone, including the CEO, now needs to take ownership and accountability over the security of important information. It is a company problem. The consensus building points I discussed in chapter 8 will help you bring all this together.

Regardless of the hacker's motivation, the consequences are the same – lost business, damaged reputation and a wide variety of immediate and longer-term expenses. With the number of data breaches continuing to grow, businesses can no longer hope that any incidents will go unnoticed. Consumers, organisations and investors are more sensitive than ever about the safety of personal data and it will take a huge amount of work for firms to regain trust in the wake of a breach. You only have to take a brief look in the media to find examples of security warnings being repeatedly ignore by all facets of the organisations – leading to one outcome – a breach.

Throughout this book, I have talked about how the balance can be struck between security and freedom by detailing best practices derived from years of experience in assisting thousands of customers across millions of endpoints. These have included best practices for designing, planning, implementation and the ongoing maintenance of a DiD project, which combines three key concepts; privilege management, application control, and content isolation. Additionally I have provided the pros and cons for a number of technologies typically used to attempt to solve the challenges in the areas discussed here. This enables you to go into this project better informed and provides the security foundations from which your environment can be built.

Partner with a solutions provider that has experience in the space and who understands the right way and the wrong way to deploy DiD. When discussing your project with the vendor, ensure he is talking in terms of project success and not simply focusing on the solution. The vendor should place significant emphasis on the design and planning stages of an implementation. Review implementation experience, reference calls and case studies to ascertain what their background is. The right solution is crucial, but you also need to be able to operationalise it, which is the difference between success and failure.

Key takeaways
1. Join up the dots between teams to truly establish your need state.
2. The threat landscape changes continually, outpacing detection based solutions, so do not build your strategy on detection.
3. Proactive measures play a strong role in a cyber kill chain and are proven to work.
4. Defend against zero day and advanced threats by not repeating the mistakes of the past.
5. Do not ignore end user freedom. If security gets in the way of productivity, it will be weakened.
6. Exception handling must form a core part of your requirements, as you cannot predict the future.

7. Do not settle for average security; use it as an enabler for end user freedom.
8. Start with the end in mind – fully understand your requirements prior to starting the project.
9. Deal with conflict early in the project or it will affect your success.
10. Ensure you involve all the stakeholders from the start.
11. Do not just buy software, buy success.

This leads me to the final thing to say; by following the advice in the book, you should be able to find the elusive balance between security and freedom, to find a productive solution that works for everyone in the organisation – good luck!

Should you have questions or want to discuss the items discussed throughout this book, you can find me at:

- **Linkedin** https://uk.linkedin.com/in/andrewavanessian
- **Twitter** @AndyAvanessian
- **Email** andrew_avanessian@hotmail.com

APPENDIX

Defaut local groups in Microsoft

Group	Description	Default user rights
Administrators	Members of this group have full control of the computer, and they can assign user rights and access control permissions to users as necessary. The Administrator account is a default member of this group. When a computer is joined to a domain, the Domain Admins group is added to this group automatically. Because this group has full control of the computer, use caution when you add users to it.	• Access this computer from the network • Adjust memory quotas for a process • Allow logon locally • Allow logon through Remote Desktop Services • Back up files and directories • Bypass traverse checking • Change the system time • Change the time zone • Create a page file • Create global objects • Create symbolic links • Debug programs • Force shutdown from a remote system • Impersonate a client after authentication • Increase scheduling priority • Load and unload device drivers • Log on as a batch job • Manage auditing and security log • Modify firmware environment variables • Perform volume maintenance tasks • Profile single process • Profile system performance • Remove computer from docking station • Restore files and directories • Shut down the system • Take ownership of files or other objects

Back up Operators	Members of this group can back up and restore files on a computer, regardless of any permissions that protect those files. This is because the right to perform a back up takes precedence over all file permissions. Members of this group cannot change security settings.	• Access this computer from the network • Allow logon locally • Back up files and directories • Bypass traverse checking • Log on as a batch job • Restore files and directories • Shut down the system
Cryptographic Operators	Members of this group are authorised to perform cryptographic operations.	No default user rights
Distributed COM Users	Members of this group are allowed to start, activate, and use DCOM objects on a computer.	No default user rights
Guests	In a computer joined to the domain, members of this group have a temporary profile created at log on, and when the member logs off, the profile is deleted. Profiles in workgroup environments are not deleted. The Guest account (which is disabled by default) is also a default member of this group.	No default user rights

Guests (continued)	Members of this group will have a temporary profile created at log on, and when the member logs off, the profile will be deleted. The Guest account (which is disabled by default) is also a default member of this group.	No default user rights
IIS_IUSRS	This is a built-in group that is used by Internet Information Services (IIS).	No default user rights
Network Configuration Operators	Members of this group can make changes to TCP/IP settings, and they can renew and release TCP/IP addresses. This group has no default members.	No default user rights
Performance Log Users	Members of this group can manage performance counters, logs, and alerts on a computer — both locally and from remote clients — without being a member of the Administrators group.	No default user rights

Performance Monitor Users	Members of this group can monitor performance counters on a computer — locally and from remote clients — without being a member of the Administrators group or the Performance Log Users groups	No default user rights
Power Users	By default, members of this group have no more user rights or permissions than a standard user account. The Power Users group in previous versions of Windows was designed to give users specific administrator rights and permissions to perform common system tasks. In this version of Windows, standard user accounts inherently have the ability to perform most common configuration tasks, such as changing time zones.	No default user rights

Power Users (continued)	For legacy applications that require the same Power User rights and permissions that were present in previous versions of Windows, administrators can apply a security template that enables the Power Users group to assume the same rights and permissions that were present in previous versions of Windows.	No default user rights
Remote Desktop Users	Members of this group can log on to the computer remotely.	Allow logon through Remote Desktop Services
Replicator	This group supports replication functions. The only member of the Replicator group should be a domain user account that is used to log on the Replicator services of a domain controller. Do not add user accounts of actual users to this group.	No default user rights

Users	Members of this group can perform common tasks, such as running applications, using local and network printers, and locking the computer. Members of this group cannot share directories or create local printers. By default, the Domain Users, Authenticated Users, and Interactive groups are members of this group. Therefore, any user account that is created in the domain becomes a member of this group.	Access this computer from the network Allow logon locally Bypass traverse checking Change the time zone Increase a process working set Remove the computer from a docking station Shut down the system
Offer Remote Assistance Helpers	Members of this group can offer Remote Assistance to the users of this computer.	No default user rights

FINAL THOUGHTS

© Andrew Avanessian 2016

ISBN: 978-1-326-79683-9

www.ingramcontent.com/pod-product-compliance
Lightning Source LLC
Chambersburg PA
CBHW060832170526
45158CB00001B/146